SOUL SEARCH

SOUL
SEARCH

*A Scientist Explores
the Afterlife*

DAVID DARLING

Villard Books New York 1995

Library of Congress Cataloging-in-Publication Data

Darling, David J.
Soul search: A scientist explores the afterlife / by David
Darling.
p.   cm.
Includes bibliographical references
ISBN 0-679-41845-8
1. Death.   2. Future life.   3. Immortality (Philosophy)
I. Title.
BD444.D32   1995   129—dc20   94-12489

Manufactured in the United States of America on acid-free
paper

9   8   7   6   5   4   3   2

First Edition

BOOK DESIGN BY LILLY LANGOTSKY

TO JILL,
NOW AND ALWAYS

"Let us deprive death of its strangeness, let us frequent it, let us get used to it; let us have nothing more often in mind than death . . . We do not know where death awaits us: so let us wait for it everywhere. To practice death is to practice freedom."

—*Michel de Montaigne*

"A wise man's life is all one preparation for death."

—*Cicero*

Acknowledgments

Once again, it is a pleasure to thank Patricia Van der Leun, my agent extraordinaire, for helping transform an idea into a book.

I am grateful, too, to Emily Bestler, my editor at Villard, for providing such excellent support and advice at every stage.

Finally, as always, none of this would have been possible without my family, who supplied the love and encouragement.

Contents

THE END

"The event of death is always astounding; our philosophy never reaches, never possesses it; we are always at the beginning of our catechism; always the definition is yet to be made. What is death?"

—*Ralph Waldo Emerson*

*W*hat happens when we die? Does everything we are just stop? Is consciousness lost forever? Or does some vital spark inside us, a spirit or a soul, live on?

We find it almost impossible to think about not having a mind, of our awareness being snuffed out like a candle. Yet the stark fact is that within a century or so, everyone alive today—all 6 billion of us—will be dead. Nothing in life is more certain. Sooner or later, whatever we do, whatever we achieve, our physical remains will be rotting in the ground or have been burned to ashes. Or perhaps like Einstein's brain, blanched bits of us will be languishing in formaldehyde, pickled for posterity and science.

We look around for comfort. But the message from the front line of brain research could hardly be more bleak. We should not build up any hope, it tells us, of being able to carry on after death. The brain too obviously plays a master role in making us what we are. When its workings are impaired, by drink, drugs or disease, "we" alter too. And when the higher centers of the brain are completely put out of action, by a knock on the head or general anesthesia, our whole inner self seems temporarily to wink out. During life, our memories, personality and awareness seem to depend crucially on the state of that bizarre, tofulike mass between our ears. Why, then, should we kid ourselves? What is the point of holding out hope of being able to think and remain conscious when the brain is dead, if we can't even do it in the depths of sleep?

Humans are the only creatures on earth that know they are going to die. But that foreknowledge has come fairly recently and it flies in the face of 4 billion years of evolution. Those eons have genetically conditioned us to do all we can to preserve ourselves and our kin. The result is that we are caught in a dilemma. We are programmed to survive by our genes yet made painfully aware of our mortality by our forward-looking brain. If we admit that death is inevitable, then our will to survive may be fatally weakened. On the other hand, if we deny death, we have to turn a blind eye to a patent fact of the real world.

Only one avenue of escape is possible—belief in an afterlife. With this we can face the nightmare that death poses to the rational mind.

Cults to do with souls and immortality have cropped up everywhere in human time and space. As far back as Neolithic times and possibly earlier, men put faith in the survival of the spirit beyond death. Archaeologists have found that early men buried food and weapons with their dead comrades to equip them for the life to come. In caves in Israel, Neanderthal remains up to 100,000 years old have been unearthed amid evidence of ritual burial. These include the skeleton of a thirteen-year-old boy found in a cavity cut into the rock at Qafzeh. The boy's body had been laid on its back with the skull resting on the grave's wall. His hands were facing upward. Across the hands and upper chest had been carefully placed the large antler of a fallow deer. In the Shanidar cave in the mountains of Iraq, a male skeleton was found lying on its side. Lining the grave were traces of ritually scattered flower petals.

From prehistory to the present day, we have countered the brevity of earthly life with the dream of eternity. Great systems of religion have sprung up to serve as focal points for our faith. But today, these traditional teachings and our cherished belief in an afterlife—what Sigmund Freud called the "oldest, strongest and most insistent wish of mankind"—are under threat. Gods and souls seem out of place in the sterile, machinelike universe shown to us by science.

As the taproot belief in our spiritual nature withers, so we go to increasing lengths to deny or fictionalize death. Death has replaced sex as the big taboo. Even mentioning it is tantamount to bad taste, and when it strikes close to home we treat it as an outrage. The loved one was "struck down," we say, as if it were somehow unnatural to die. Freud pointed out that when a death occurs, "Our habit is to lay stress on the fortuitous causation of the death—accident, disease, infection, advanced age; in this way we betray an effort to reduce death from a necessity to a chance event."

We distance ourselves from death by institutionalizing it. Whereas in earlier times most people spent their last days at home in the bosom of family and friends, today four-fifths of us are removed to hospitals or nursing homes. We are hidden from the gaze of the young and healthy and tended to by strangers. As the end approaches, we are discreetly moved to wards for the terminally ill and plugged into life-support machines. Technology takes over. And when we do eventually die, it is often the inadequacy of the equipment or the shortcomings of the treatment that are blamed.

Instead of accepting death as a natural and inevitable fact of life, we are in danger of convincing ourselves that, given further medical advances, we shall be able to stave it off for as long as we like. "Some people want to achieve immortality through their works or their descendants," said Woody Allen. "I want to achieve it through not dying." Now, for the first time, science seems to be holding out the slender hope of cheating death. Already, some of our vital parts can be replaced with natural or synthetic substitutes. In time, it seems, the transplant surgeon will be able to do for a human being what any competent mechanic in a well-equipped garage can do for a car.

On a different front, the search is on for ways to slow or halt the steady degeneration of our bodies. Immortality without death beckons. Perhaps within the next century, we are told, genuine elixirs of life will be as freely available in drugstores as vitamin pills are today. Then the old alchemists' dream will have come true and, along with our weekly groceries, we will bring home the means to slow or even reverse our aging processes.

Some of us may not live long enough to benefit from such advances. But no matter. For a price, we can arrange to have our still-fresh remains deeply frozen— our whole body, or merely our head (a "neuro"), stored like a pickle in liquid nitrogen—to await the glorious day when technology may be able to restore us to life. How desperate can we get? British biologists Peter and Jean Medawar voiced what must be the opinion of most rationally minded folk: "In our opinion, money invested to preserve human life in the deep freeze is money wasted, the sums involved being large enough to fulfill a punitive function as a self-imposed fine for gullibility and vanity."

Danger signs are looming; we are becoming increasingly obsessed with clinging to life, avoiding death, at any cost. And not just our dignity is at stake. We have lost touch with the natural world and our spiritual roots. No longer is there a sense of participation in the living cycle, the renewing, regenerative sequence of life-to-death-to-life. Western man has wandered into a spiritual desert where traditions of intimacy with nature, the final rite of passage, and the belief in an eternal life have all but been forgotten.

We fear death for many reasons. We fear the possibility of pain because we see it in the faces of others, the agony and angst of terminal cancer. We fear death's unpredictability, its awesome power to bring in an instant an end to everything we have lived and worked for. We fear the death of loved ones—parents, spouses and children. But above all we fear the loss of ourselves.

In the words of Sogyal Rinpoche, one of today's leading exponents of Tibetan Buddhism:

> . . . our instinctive desire is to live and to go on living, and death is a savage end to everything we hold familiar. We feel that when it comes we will be plunged into something quite unknown, or become someone totally different. We imagine we will find ourselves lost and bewildered, in surroundings that are terrifyingly unfamiliar. We imagine it will be like waking up alone, in a torment of anxiety, in a foreign country, with no knowledge of the land or language, no money, no contacts, no passport, no friends . . .

As much as we believe anything, we believe that we have a unique, personal "self," an inner "I," that must be preserved at all cost. But if we dare to look deeply into this being, we find it is made up of no more than baggage picked up along life's way: a name tag, a character and biography shaped by our dealings with other people, memories of past events, possessions, family and friends, a hometown and everything else we have chanced across and claimed as "our own." These are the fragile props on which we depend and to which we desperately cling. Death is feared because it means a certain end to them all and, therefore, to the person we mistook them for. Sogyal Rinpoche points out: "We live under an assumed identity, in a neurotic fairy tale world with no more reality than the Mock Turtle in *Alice in Wonderland*. Hypnotized by the thrill of building, we have raised the houses of our lives on sand. This world can seem marvelously convincing until death collapses the illusion and evicts us from our hiding place."

"You can't take it with you," the saying goes. No, but you can't take "you" with you, either. And that is the prime source of our death fear.

What, then, can we hope for after death? Nothing— absolutely nothing—if we believe what many scientists say. All life, they argue, can be understood in terms of chemical reactions. Every event, all the wonders of nature, can be explained by the accidental bumping and jiggling of particles. The brain *is* the mind. Why trouble to speculate further about an immaterial soul or afterlife?

We have come to respect the judgment of scientists on almost every issue because science works so well. It makes progress. It tells us in greater and greater detail how atoms behave or the universe has evolved. It gives us a privileged glimpse at the mathematical script that nature follows. And, most visibly to the ordinary person, it leads to all kinds of technological marvels that have transformed our lives.

In effect, science has usurped religion and scientists have become our new high priests. The problem is that when science takes on spiritual or moral issues, it is an unmitigated disaster. To science, a human being is no more than a complicated machine. And how can a machine have a soul? The respected neurologist Richard Restak has even gone so far as to try to find evidence for the human soul by peering into brains with a PET scanner. Needless to say, he has come up empty-handed.

As a society, we have made the mistake of thinking that because science can answer some questions very well, it might eventually be able to answer *all* questions. Scientists used to be quite modest in their claims. But recently a number of them have been growing more ambitious, as if the illusory power we have handed them has affected their judgment. The result has been a number of grandiose claims that can be neither justified nor fulfilled. For example, Steven Hawking ended his book *A Brief History of Time* with the statement that if his theory about the nature of the universe was upheld, it would help us "know the mind of God.'' Hawking may be a genius, but his opinions about God carry no more weight than those of his next-door neighbor. In a similar forthright style, Oxford evolutionary-biologist Richard Dawkins, author of *The Selfish Gene,* has said: ''Science offers us an explanation of how complexity arose out of simplicity. The hypothesis of God offers no worthwhile explanation for anything . . . We cannot prove there is no God, but we can safely conclude that He is very, very improbable indeed.''

Dawkins may draw what conclusions he likes. But others may feel his aggressive intolerance of religion smacks of the very dogma he is so anxious to avoid. It is not hard to see why reductionism fails to find a God or a soul, or even a subjective aspect to human experience. All of these are left out of the reductionist's agenda from the very start.

In approaching issues such as death and the afterlife, an open mind and tolerance for all viewpoints are essential. We need to look through the eyes of the scientist and of the mystic and learn what we can from both. In doing this, we shall simply be following the lead of some of the world's truly great thinkers.

Men of the stature of Niels Bohr and Albert Einstein were well aware of a link between their own work and long-held mystical traditions. Bohr, the most influential of all the pioneers of quantum mechanics, once said: ''For a parallel to the lesson of atomic theory . . . [we must turn] to those kinds of epistemological problems with which already thinkers like the Buddha and Lao

Tzu have been confronted, when trying to harmonize our position as spectators and actors in the great drama of existence.''

Likewise, the present Dalai Lama sees the possibility for much bridge-building between science and more intuitive forms of knowledge. He writes: ''Death and Dying provide a meeting point between the Tibetan Buddhist and modern scientific traditions. I believe both have a great deal to contribute to each other on the level of understanding and of practical benefit.''

Science would never make a good religion. By its very nature, it is chained to the material and the measurable. Far too much will always slip through its net. But because of what has recently been discovered about the world, scientists are at least being encouraged to think a little more holistically. For instance, there have been some momentous changes in the way science regards complicated systems. These are systems that, although made up of elements obeying fixed laws, are made up of so many elements that those laws are lost in a blizzard of complexity. Living organisms, it turns out, cannot even in principle be fully understood in terms of the separate particles of which they are composed. Even on a material level, we are more than just the sum of our microscopic parts.

Scientists have also had to revise drastically their view of man's relationship to the universe. From the physics of the subatomic world, quantum mechanics, we have learned that it may be meaningless to talk about the existence of particles outside of our observations. It appears that by interrogating nature at the finest level we actually play a decisive part in bringing some aspects of reality into being.

Reductionism had effectively cut man off from the universe. It had become part of the scientific canon that the experiences of human beings were somehow of a lower order of reality than were events "outside." But now, quantum mechanics insists we can no longer hold with that duality. The fleeting particles that pop up in laboratory experiments owe their brief lives to the researchers who observe them. The particles are not always there, waiting to be noticed. They are provoked into existence from the shadowy quantum realm where nothing is solid or defined. The boundary between subject and object has become blurred.

On a cosmic scale, too, we have suddenly and unexpectedly found ourselves thrust into the limelight. It turns out that we live in a universe unreasonably well suited to the development of life. About 15 billion years ago, space, time, matter and energy came into being in a titanic explosion known as the Big Bang. Our presence here today rests on that outburst having been precisely as violent as it was; even a slight tampering with the size of the bang would have caused the universe either to fly apart or fall back on itself before stars, planets and life had a chance to form. Other uncanny coincidences have been found in the relative strengths of the four basic forces in nature and in the particular location of energy levels in key atoms such as carbon and oxygen. Wherever we look, whenever we look, we find that nature is strangely sympathetic to the evolution of life and intelligence.

These new perspectives of the world have not really brought a spiritual dimension to science. That would be claiming too much. But they have allowed the gap between the spiritual and the material to close. We are beginning to see that we are written into the narrative of nature in a fundamental and mysterious way. Mind is not just something existing in a void playing with neutral items and trying to fit them into a vapid theory; rather it "belongs" in the universe. The new scientific picture, with its holistic overtones, sits better too with intuitive ideas such as reverence for the soil, water and air. It is in keeping with a sense of the sacred and a wordless feeling that we are an integral, inseparable part of all that exists.

Nature, we now appreciate, is an elegant unity whether we care to survey the macrocosm of the stars and galaxies or the microcosm of the atom. And we, it seems, may have a role—perhaps a very profound role—to play in this unfolding drama. The universe we find ourselves in is an evolving web of space-time that has spawned everything from particles to people, from quarks to consciousness.

Now the time has come to broaden our field of inquiry. In turning to face the deeper mysteries of life and death, we need to embrace not just what is outside us, but also what is within. As Tolstoy wrote: "The highest wisdom has but one science, the science of the whole, the science explaining the Creation and man's place in it.''

We wonder what is the purpose of life and why we have to die. But science has shown us that life and death, in the broadest sense, are all around us. We exist today because, billions of years ago, giant stars ''lived'' and ''died'' in great explosions that threw out the fusion-made heavy elements of which our bodies are composed. Only by living and dying have plants and animals been able to evolve into such complex forms as ourselves. Only by living and dying do other life-forms continue to provide us with food and oxygen. And only by living and dying ourselves do we contribute in some small way to the process of universal recycling.

The simple truth is, there could not be a you, and there could not be a viable universe, without death—the death of stars and the death of succeeding generations of organic life. In the words of philosopher John Bowker:

If you ask, ''Why is death happening to me (or to anyone)?'' the answer is: because the universe is happening to you; you are an event of the universe; you are a child of the stars, as well as of your parents, and you could not be a child in any other way. Even while you live, and certainly when you die, the atoms and molecules which are at present locked into your shape and appearance are being unlocked and scattered into other shapes and forms of construction.

We know that our bodies will eventually decay. We know that our brains will stop working. The great question remains whether consciousness is similarly doomed. Is there, as we so desperately want to believe, an afterlife waiting for us beyond the gates of death? The answer, I believe, is within our grasp.

As some scientists peer into the innermost recesses of the human brain, others continue to refine our knowledge of the near-death experience. Clues to the nature and future of consciousness are being supplied by fields as diverse as neurology, psychology, cosmology and quantum physics. And added to all this is a growing sense that a merger between the highest teachings of science, religion and mysticism is long overdue—a grand synthesis that will finally help us solve the greatest mystery in the universe.

SOUL SEARCH

DEATH COMES OF AGE

"Man has given a false importance to death. Any animal, plant or man who dies adds to Nature's compost heap, becomes the manure without which nothing could grow, nothing could be created. Death is simply part of the process."

—*Peter Weiss, German dramatist and novelist*

$\mathcal{D}$eath seems certain and universal. So the shock is all the greater when we find all around us swarms of living things that never show the slightest signs of aging.

Bacteria, for instance, don't grow old in the normal sense. They can be killed by extremes of heat, toxic chemicals, viruses and the like. But they never succumb to old age. Not for them the creeping senility, inevitable among our own species, as tissues and organs wear out and fail. Bacteria grow, but in growing retain their pristine form and perfectly running cellular machinery—right up to the point at which they neatly divide down the middle and become two.

We are not used to thinking about this kind of reproduction. Conceptual problems spring to mind. If bacteria don't age or die, then what exactly *does* happen at the moment they divide? In the human world we can keep track of individuals and their parents and offspring. But with bacteria, matters are not so clear-cut. When a mother cell divides, the old organism vanishes on the spot, to be replaced by two smaller, genetically identical copies. The parent organism in effect *becomes* its offspring; those offspring in turn become their own daughters, and so it goes on. The upshot is that, barring any random genetic changes, the family tree of a colony of bacteria has no distinguishable branches or lineages. It just telescopes down to a single anonymous member, an endlessly fragmenting, endlessly rejuvenating progenitor.

Given such a reproductive style, it is hard to say whether bacteria really qualify as "individuals." On the one hand, a single microbe can be isolated and thought of as a creature apart (at least until it becomes two). On the other hand, there is no practical way to distinguish this cell from any of the others in the colony. All are clones. And, when it eventually does divide, where on earth does our supposed individual go?

Such habitually dividing organisms as bacteria are ageless in the sense that they show no signs of deterioration as time goes by. But agelessness is not the same thing as immortality, because to be immortal a creature has to preserve its individuality—its "personal" continuity—in some recognizable form.

Are there any such genuinely eternal life-forms on earth? Probably not, but the best candidates are organisms such as brewers' and bakers' yeasts. These are fungi that multiply by budding, so that the daughter cells are clearly distinguishable and chronologically younger than those of the mother. Since new buds can't form at the site of old bud scars, the mother eventually becomes sterile: after about twenty buddings it is peppered with scars and can no longer bear offspring. Budding bacteria exist, too. The photosynthetic bacterium *Rhodopseudomonas palustris* seems to sprout daughters with impunity, as do certain bacteria that grow on stalks. All these microscopic budding life-forms show definite mother-daughter relationships in their reproduction. What is not clear is whether the mother, after it ceases to bud, eventually dies. The general assumption is that it does. But, in fact, there is no firm evidence for this and it remains a tantalizing possibility that budding microbes represent the only genuinely immortal beings on the planet.

Back, though, to simple splitting cells. These we can be sure are at least ageless. But why? Human beings age. Virtually every life-form we can see with the unaided eye (the giant amoeba is an exception) ages as time goes by. We grow, our bodies slowly wear out, and we die. So why, if eternal youth is a birthright of the simplest living things, is it so manifestly denied to more advanced creatures like ourselves? Why are human cells, and the complex beings they are shaped into, apparently predestined to die?

Despite all the great strides made by medical science, most of us will be lucky to survive much beyond the biblical three score and ten years. Improvements in hygiene and the treatment of disease have done wonders for the quality of our lives. They have dramatically reduced our chances of an early death through illness. But even in the most developed nations (Japan and Sweden currently head the longevity league), the average life span of men and women has yet to rise above eighty. Nor, barring some revolution in gerontology, can we expect any sudden upswing in progress in the near future. Eliminating every major pathological cause of death today, including the three biggest killers, cancer, heart disease and strokes, would still leave the normal upper limit of human life stuck at around ninety or one hundred years. It is as if each of us harbors a time bomb, primed at birth, that relentlessly marks off the seconds before we die.

We are all composed of cells—roughly 100 trillion of them. But with certain exceptions, most notably the neurons of the brain, the cells making up your body now are not the same as those that were inside you a few years ago. This is equally true of other multicellular organisms. It is an often-repeated "fact" that bristlecone pines and sequoias are among the oldest living things on earth. And in one respect this is true: the eldest of these venerable plants began life well before the Roman Empire reached its heyday. On the other hand, no living cell inside any of these ancient trees today is more than thirty years old—less than a third of the age of the oldest living nerve cells inside some human beings. So, if we take only *living* cells as a measure of an organism's age, then it is we, not the bristlecones, who rank among the world's extreme geriatrics.

As each of our body cells dies, it is replaced by another and that one by another and so on. The trouble is, this process of substitution and replication does not go on forever. The root of the problem was uncovered by the American biologists Leonard Hayflick and Paul Moorhead at the Wistar Institute in 1961. Hayflick and Moorhead demonstrated the reality of a time fuse in man by teasing cells from soft body tissue and allowing them to grow in a culture fluid. Working with human fibroblasts (connective-tissue cells) taken from embryos, they found that there is a definite limit to the number of times these cells will divide. Over a period of months, the cells in each culture divided repeatedly, gradually slowed down in their rate of reproduction, became visibly sick and, after a total of about fifty divisions, died.

Later experiments showed that normal cells apparently have a mechanism somewhere inside the nucleus for remembering the number of times they have divided. What is more, this "memory" survives even in cells that have been stored for long periods at very low temperatures in liquid nitrogen. Frozen at the twentieth doubling, for instance, the cells undergo thirty more doublings after being thawed, and then stop. Frozen at the tenth doubling they oblige with forty more, and then die. Always the total is around fifty. One particular strain studied by Hayflick kept accurate count of its number of doublings even after being stored for more than thirteen years at −190°C.

No exception has yet been found to the rule that normal cells have a finite capacity to divide, as measured by the so-called Hayflick limit. In other animals, the limit is different: about twenty in the mouse, twenty-five in the chicken and 110 in that most long-lived of vertebrates, the Galápagos tortoise. The longer the natural life span of the organism, the higher its Hayflick limit—which seems reasonable. Less obvious is why there should be any restriction at all on how many times a normal cell can reproduce.

Intriguingly, this doubling limit does not apply to certain other types of cells. Cancer cells and germ-line cells (eggs and sperm) in particular appear to be immune to aging. These are the jokers in the pack; both types can and do divide endlessly without showing any signs of wear and tear. A cancer cell looks abnormal and divides abnormally: chaotically and dangerously. A normal cell infected with a cancer-causing virus, as Hayflick showed, becomes cancerous and will subsequently divide without limit in a maintained laboratory culture. It seems ironic that for ordinary animal cells to aspire to immortality they should have to take on some of the very properties that would cause the eventual demise of their host organism—and, therefore, of themselves.

Egg and sperm cells, too, have the potential for immortality, a fact first noted as long ago as 1885 by the great German biologist August Weismann. Weismann drew a clear distinction between what he called the human "germ-plasm," the chromosomal material involved in reproduction, and the rest of the body, or "soma." In the light of this distinction, we can think about the problem of the origin of death in another way. That is, why has nature engineered a fundamental difference between cells that are ageless and those that form a mere temporary and disposable receptacle? Obviously, if we and other organisms never died, evolution would have been impossible, and we would not be here to ponder the riddle of our own mortality. But that is an argument based on hindsight. We need to avoid the suggestion that nature somehow had it in mind all along to make complex throwaway life-forms. Biological evolution, blind and undirected, simply doesn't work that way.

Instead, we need to seek out the origins of human mortality at a molecular level. The secret of the birth of death almost certainly lies among the tangled braids of that peculiar and unique substance, deoxyribonucleic acid—DNA. One of the outstanding achievements of twentieth-century science has been the elucidation of DNA's molecular structure. The now-familiar double helix arrangement of DNA resembles nothing so much as a twisted rope ladder. The rungs consist of chemicals, known as amino-acid bases, which are code named *A* (for adenine), *G* (for guanine), *T* (for thymine) and *C* (for cytosine). These bases are effectively the four letters in the alphabet of life. Just as we use the twenty-six letters of the English alphabet to construct specific messages and meanings, so nature casts the four amino-acid bases into sequences that carry specific biological information. Genes are simply long lists of instructions rendered in the four-symbol alphabet of DNA, each gene specifying the design of a particular product, usually a protein.

The bases that compose these genetic messages have a very special property which is at the core of life on earth—they always pair in the same way, *A* with *T*, and *G* with *C*. As a result, the rungs of the DNA ladder consist of *A-T* and *G-C* pairs. Crucially, these pairs are structurally interchangeable so that, for instance, a *C-G* pair can substitute for an *A-T* pair without disturbing the shape or stability of the DNA spiral. Holding each rung together at its midpoint is a weak chemical bond (a hydrogen bond) that is easily broken when the time comes for the DNA to divide and unravel into separate strands.

During cell division, when the double helix of DNA peels apart, two copies of the original genetic message are created. Although equivalent, these copies are not identical. One is the complement of the other, just as a mold and a cast contain the same image but in inverted forms. For example, if the base sequence on one side of the divided DNA ladder is *AAGCTATCCG,* the sequence on the complementary side will be *TTCGAT-AGGC.*

Imagine that, for some reason, a mistake creeps in during the copying process. A *G,* say, couples with an *A* instead of a *C.* Now, after the partner strands have separated following replication, one strand will have the correct base (*G*) and the other a mistake (*A*). Because the coupling rules are extremely unlikely to be broken twice in succession, the outcome of the next round of copying is almost inevitably one offspring DNA with a (correct) *G-C* pair and one with an (incorrect) *A-T* pair. At first sight, it seems as if this mismatching might have disastrous consequences, perhaps throwing the whole DNA molecule into disarray. However, since the *A-T* pair has the same basic symmetry as the *G-C* pair, each new DNA will preserve the original 3-D helical format. An error has found its way into the code but the architecture of the code's carrier, DNA, remains uncompromised.

In DNA, alone among known copying machines, order is preserved in the face of random mistakes, not destroyed by them. Yet the ceaseless editing and proofreading needed to root out occasional duplication errors do not come free. They take up a sizable slice of the cell's total energy budget. Further energy has to be channeled into keeping the cell's life functions running smoothly. Damaged proteins must be quickly tracked down and disposed of before they can wreak havoc; energy has to be diverted to the machinery that monitors the efficiency of the cell's protein-making processes, and so on.

Primitive, one-celled creatures such as bacteria can easily come up with the energy required for damage control, because they are genetically and functionally simple. But with bigger and more elaborate organisms, maintaining error-free copying is more of a problem. The trouble is that tying up too many resources in genetic error-checking makes the creature less viable in other ways. Little is to be gained from having a high-accuracy body if it is defenseless against low-accuracy, short-lived predators. In any case, argue biologists Thomas Kirkwood of the Medical Research Council in London and Richard Cutler of the National Institute on Aging in Baltimore, why waste energy trying to preserve immortality when an individual is likely to be killed by environmental hazards within a fairly short and predictable period anyway? From nature's point of view, it makes more sense to invest in protective systems that ensure youthful vigor for a certain amount of time and no longer. The rest of the organism's energy can then go toward maximizing fertility—which is the main goal of the exercise.

Kirkwood calls his model the disposable soma theory and likens it to industry's practice of investing little in the durability of goods that will be used for only a limited time. In an organism's case it is the somatic cells—the nonreproductive cells making up the bulk of the body—that are eventually expendable. In contrast, germ-line cells, occurring in tissues that give rise to eggs and sperm, must retain the ability to repair themselves perfectly, otherwise the species would die out. Because genes in germ-line cells account for only a tiny fraction (typically less than 1 percent) of total body genes, the cost of maintaining high-precision error-correcting processes in the ovaries and testes is tolerably low.

At some stage in the dim past, then, it seems that evolution stumbled upon a novel solution to the problem of reproduction. It put immortal, ''selfish'' genes in disposable shells. This was the successful formula that led to all of the more complex life-forms on earth—including man.

But with the evolution of ourselves there arose a special and unique complication. The perishable machine built by human genes contains the most highly developed brain we know. This brain, like the rest of the body, has a finite life span. Yet it is also the vehicle for our indomitable sense of self.

Man's brain was the first on this planet to be able to project its thoughts into the future, to be able to predict events based upon experience. So, inevitably, it was also the first brain to be able to foresee its own end. That was the tragedy in the tale of the fall from Eden: with the birth of the ego, death entered our consciousness.

Death is not nearly so old as life, but self-consciousness and the fear of death is much younger still. Other animals appear not to have these in any developed form at all, and even man, some circumstantial evidence suggests, may not always have enjoyed full self-awareness as we know it today.

From prehistoric remains it is hard, and perhaps

unrealistic, to try to reconstruct the mental and spiritual worlds of our long-dead ancestors. All our theories are bound to be parochial, tainted as they are by present-day attitudes and beliefs. Fortunately, though, we have more than just fossil evidence to go by. There are folk still alive today who almost certainly preserve, in both their memories and traditions, the essence of Neolithic man.

For at least forty thousand years the Aborigines have lived in Australia and for almost all that time they have practiced the hunter-gatherer lifestyle once common to all men. Although during this century they have become permanently settled, their surviving languages and customs serve as an extraordinary window on the remote past.

That window is not always very clear. We forget sometimes that there are ways of thinking, ways of interpreting the world, that are totally alien to our own, and the truth is that the intricacies of Aboriginal traditions are often hard for Westerners to follow. But a striking feature of native Australians that does come through is their attitude toward self. Aborigines—certainly pre-European Aborigines—were far less concerned with thoughts about their personal identities than about their relationship with the land and with other living things around them. Individuals saw themselves as part of a vast, unchanging, interconnected system. They considered themselves not simply in terms of bloodlines or families, but as deeply and inseparably connected with the wider context of the social group and, beyond that, the whole mythical structure of life. All the evidence suggests that Aboriginal consciousness was, and to some extent still is, collective and communal.

Time also seems to be perceived quite differently in the Aboriginal world. To the Aborigine, time appears cyclical rather than linear, because life itself is cyclical. The grass sprouts in the spring, grows green in the summer, withers in the autumn, dies in the winter, but always returns again the following year. This is the invariably observed pattern, the wheel of nature turning round and round. And because, to the Aborigine, Man himself is an integral part of nature, he too must participate in the recycling process. In the deepest sense, the Aborigine has no fear of death because, as far as he or she is concerned, nothing ever dies.

Death, or at least our perception of it, is something relatively new. We think of death as being tragic, terrifying, even repugnant. But it has none of those qualities if you see it every day in a natural context, if you hunt and collect your own food, if you are continuously in touch with the cycle of the seasons. Primitive men and women considered themselves inseparable elements—cells as it were—of a social organism: a Gaean entity whose life continued out of an indefinite past and into an indefinite future. What we know today as the soul was, judging by the prevailing beliefs of primitive people now, originally thought of as a larger life embodied in the successive members of the group. At death, this personalized life simply returned like a river to the collective tribal sea.

For virtually all of human history, a span of between

2 million and 3 million years, it has been this way. The rights of the individual have been secondary to the rights of the group. The consciousness of the individual has been subordinate to the unitary, indestructible consciousness of the tribe.

Then, at some point less than ten thousand years ago, there came a change. Man began to build settlements as he learned to cultivate crops and domesticate animals. He erected walls and cities to protect himself and his property. And at the same time it seems that the beam down which man looked out on the world became more and more tightly focused. Nature became detached, something "out there." The tribal links were weakened and, we may conjecture, consciousness increasingly withdrew into the individual. To a greater extent perhaps than ever before, people became preoccupied by their personal sense of self and with a new and terrible image: the specter of death.

How sudden and recent was this subtle shift in the location of consciousness, from the collective to the individual? In a highly controversial thesis, first published in 1977, Princeton psychologist Julian Jaynes proposed that self-awareness was still only partially developed as late as the second millennium B.C. Jaynes based his claim on analysis of several important ancient texts, including Homer's *Iliad,* written about three thousand years ago. In these he found no reference to minds, thoughts, feelings—or to self. He concluded, therefore, that the people of this time did not recognize their thoughts and actions as their own but believed instead that they emanated from the gods. As an example, he cited an episode from the *Iliad* concerning the Greek hero Achilles. One god makes Achilles promise not to go into battle against the Trojans, another urges him on, and yet another screams through Achilles' throat at the enemies. Homer portrays mighty Achilles as if he were a puppet dancing to the thoughts and wills of higher minds.

It might well be argued, of course, that Homer intended his story to be interpreted this way: as a conflict fought out not just between men but also between the Olympian gods acting through men. After all, there is nothing new in the idea that men sometimes act of their own free will and at other times are driven to certain actions by circumstances beyond their control. While Jaynes's thesis is intriguing, it is far from convincing. He puts the birth of self-awareness at some point after 1000 B.C., but in all likelihood it happened very much earlier.

The emergence of a sense of self was surely a gradual process influenced by both biological and cultural factors. It takes a brain of a certain size and complexity—though not necessarily a human brain—to subtend a sophisticated sense of self. But the blossoming of that sense of self can take place only in the right environment—an environment in which your fellows relate to you (and you to them) as if you were a free-thinking individual in your own right.

This suggests that the evolution of self-awareness and that of language were strongly intertwined. Only through language are we able to break the world down into parts, to name objects and their interrelationships. Eventually, as part of this labeling, parsing process, we must have come to see ourselves as separate beings with separate, distinct minds.

The dawning of self-awareness in a form we would now recognize probably came while there were still quite primitive spoken tongues. Yet with speech the emphasis is on interaction with others, on the communal sharing of information. The only time that speaking throws the self into sharp relief (internally) is when we talk alone. Self-consciousness seems to go hand-in-hand with the ability to hold a one-man conversation. So, conceivably, the later stages in the growth of self-consciousness were encouraged by instances when some of our Stone Age forebears turned around to find that the person they had been talking to was no longer there.

Writing, too, when at last it appeared, may have played a part in the final honing of an awareness of self. Whereas spoken language is generally communal, written language is invariably personal. The only interpreter of a given sequence of written symbols is the mind that scans it, so that reading is essentially a self-conversation between the individual and the text. For the writer, the sense of self is further emphasized because the mind that is writing has to build consciously an external representation of its own internal workings.

Self-consciousness surely evolved, for the most part,

very gradually. There were no instantaneous break-throughs, no one who woke up and for the first time in the history of the world thought of himself as "I." We cannot even quantify or make comparisons concerning consciousness as we can, for instance, the cranial capacity of modern man and his ancestors. So, inevitably, all our proposals about how and when the various stages of awareness arose are purely conjectural.

Yet that does not make the guessing game any less intriguing. We know that self-consciousness has grown: a mouse is manifestly more self-aware than a minnow; we are more self-aware than a monkey. So it is pertinent to ask whether there were indeed periods in prehistory and history when man's view of the world and of himself evolved faster than usual. A tenuous clue, perhaps, comes from the Sumerian folk legend known as the Epic of Gilgamesh, which in its oldest surviving form comes to us on twelve five-thousand-year-old clay tablets from the library of Ashurnasirpal at Nineveh. In this ancient tale we read that the death of Gilgamesh's companion, Enkidu, has stunned the hero. Gilgamesh laments: "Enkidu, I weep for you like a wailing woman. You were the axe by my side, the sword in my belt, the shield before me. I also will die and worms will eat my flesh. I now fear death and have lost all my courage."

It is the man, the self-aware ego, that is lamenting here. And we are left with the impression that his grief reflects a newly acquired and painful sense of personal isolation in the people in general of this time. The myth goes on to tell how Gilgamesh, by performing certain rituals, wins permission from the gods of the underworld for the spirit of Enkidu to return to tell him about the state of the dead. Enkidu speaks of a House of Darkness in which the inhabitants are compelled to stay forever, feeding on dust and clay and wearing wings like birds for garments. And, again, we are struck by the acute loss of community, a loss tempered by a new hope—that each man and woman has an immortal spirit of his and her own. Just as the consciousness of the tribe has fragmented into separate selves within the city-state, so apparently the collective, tribal soul has been perceived as broken apart into the souls of individuals.

Opinions may differ. We may never know when and over what length of time man, unlike other animals, became fully ego-conscious. But of this we can be certain: when self-awareness *did* finally arrive it inevitably led to the quest for the survival of self after death.

2

THE QUEST FOR ETERNITY

"Neither a man nor a nation can live without a higher idea, and there is only one such idea on earth, that of an immortal human soul; all the other higher ideas by which men live follow from that."

—*Fyodor Dostoyevsky*

By 3000 B.C., the whole issue of life after death and the preservation of the soul had become of paramount concern for early pre-Western civilizations. In fact, with the emphasis now shifted to the individual and to the inescapable fact of personal death, these questions turned into an obsession. How else can we explain the astounding scale and extravagance of the Great Pyramid of Cheops? Built in 2720 B.C. from more than 2 million quarried limestone blocks with an average weight of two and a half tons, it soars 480 feet from the desert sands—a mighty challenge both to time and to death itself.

Central to the Egyptians' cult of the afterlife was the part played by mummification. Yet this process was so costly that it was not until the second millennium B.C. that the practice began to spread beyond the royal household. Since the pharaoh was the intermediary between the gods and the earth in a society where survival depended on organized agriculture, the cult was the key not only to social order but also to fertility. Therefore when the Egyptians connected their pharaoh's immortality with the cult of the god of vegetation, Osiris, they were symbolizing death and resurrection in the annual cycle of the very food they ate.

During the second millennium, the Osirian cult gained in strength, and people's views on the afterlife tended to change. While mummification implied physical immortality for the body in this world, Osiris came to be thought of as the ruler of the dead in another realm. So, increasingly, the soul was thought of as having a separate existence from the body.

According to Egyptian theology a person had not just one but two or more souls, different in nature from each other. Principally, there was the *ka,* or "guardian spirit," shown in tomb paintings as hovering over the mummy in the guise of a small bird with a human face. And there was the *ba,* or "breath," which gave animation to the body. Both the *ka* and the *ba* were thought to leave the body at death—but only temporarily. In the strange ceremony known as the Opening of the Mouth, the mouth and eyes of the

corpse were pried open by means of special instruments held by a priest. This supposedly allowed the
breath soul back into the mummy and commemorated
the myth that Osiris, after the god Seth had killed and
dismembered him, was brought back to life in the same
way by his son Horus. With the *ba* restored to its
rightful owner, it was left only for the *ka* to fly back
and reunite with its companion. This was thought to
take place in a second, parallel ceremony in the next
world. Recognition of the body by the *ka* being all-
important, it was essential for the dead person's appearance to be faithfully preserved by embalming.

Of course, we foster all kinds of romantic myths
about what the mortician-priests of Egypt did in the
cool depths of pharaonic tombs. So perhaps the truth is
bound to seem a little prosaic. Magical incantations
aside, the process of mummification was really quite
straightforward—in fact, in chemical terms, relatively
crude. The Egyptians basically salted their dead with
natron, a natural deposit found in the Nile Valley consisting chiefly of sodium carbonate and sodium bicar-
bonate (baking soda), and varying amounts of other
substances, including sodium sulphate and sodium chlo-
ride (table salt). This mixture dehydrated the corpse
and so inhibited the enzymatic activity that normally
causes decay.

At the same time, most of the internal organs were
removed, starting with the brain, which was drawn out
piecemeal through the nostrils with an iron hook and
then discarded. Viscera such as the lungs, liver and

intestines were taken out whole and stored separately in sealed canopic jars, each bearing the likeness of a particular patron god. The stomach was either removed in the same way or else flushed out with wine and filled with aromatics, while the heart was either left untouched (since it was believed to be the seat of intelligence and consciousness) or replaced with a sacred scarab. Preliminaries seen to, there followed the careful swathing of the body with bandages soaked in resins and the sprinkling with scents.

It was a lengthy procedure—in more ways than one: a mummy unwrapped in 1940 at the Metropolitan Museum of Art in New York yielded more than 850 square yards of linen. It was also a painstakingly elaborate ritual. The bandage of Nekhebt had to be placed on the well-oiled forehead, the bandage of Hathor on the face, and an impressive array of precious objects (143, in the case of Tutankhamen) at strategic positions between the wrappings. The nails were gilded, a crystal hung to lighten the face and special material applied to strengthen the steps of the deceased in the underworld. Finally, after seventy days of exhaustive preparation, the priests climaxed their work with the Opening of the Mouth.

Thus the pharaoh was made ready for his transformation into a divine and incorruptible image. Mummification and its attendant ceremonies helped ensure reunion between body and soul in the hereafter. But even with these precautions, the dead king was not guaranteed immortality. For this he still needed the compliance of the major deities. Once inside the spirit world, the deceased would be led by the jackal-headed god, Anubis, to the judgment scales, where his heart would be weighed against a feather symbolizing Maat, the goddess of justice and truth. If the scales balanced, Osiris would rule that the man had led a blameless life and so deserved to be made immortal. Conversely, if his heart proved too heavy, a less attractive fate lay in store: the unfortunate sinner would be fed to the permanently ravenous dog-monster Amemait, which lurked nearby.

It is just as well that the priests who labored so long to preserve their dead could never know what would eventually become of so many of their carefully prepared cadavers. The relatively few well-preserved mummies that have come down to us are exceptions; a great many were either burgled or bungled and long ago decayed to insect-swarming filth. Thousands of others were torn apart over the centuries to make quack cures for various ailments (the very word *mummy* comes from the Persian *mumiai,* for "pitch" or "asphalt," once thought to be a curative and for which the blackened resin of the wrappings was mistaken). Some of the ancient corpses were pulverized to produce "mummy brown" pigment for watercolor paint. And, most extraordinarily, huge numbers of mummies were used as fuel on the first Egyptian railways, their layers of resin-impregnated bandages apparently serving as an excellent substitute for coal.

Today, embalming remains a skilled and well-

practiced art. In the United States, more than 90 percent of the newly deceased go through the process. Yet
now it has come to serve a very different purpose.
Whereas in ancient Egypt the dead were preserved
exclusively for the sake of the dead and their well-
being in the hereafter, in the modern world embalming
is done nearly always for the benefit of the living. The
only exception is in the case of those individuals who
choose (and can pay in advance) to be put in a deep
freeze for possible future resuscitation or, alternatively,
to be mummified by the latest technology, which involves, in the final stages, being coated with an airtight
seal of polyurethane.

For those today who believe in an afterlife, there is a
tendency to link the notion of life after death with that
of a particular god. But theology and conjectures about
the human soul have not always gone hand in hand. In
ancient Greece, where many people eventually grew
tired of the all-too-human antics of Zeus and his cro-
nies, philosophers started to argue about the nature of
the soul from a purely academic and secular point of
view. Their approach was to travel about, look at the
world in a detached, almost arrogant sort of way, and
then theorize. The word *theory,* in fact, comes from the
Greek for "sight-seeing."

Pythagoras, in the late sixth century B.C., was the
first to establish an entire school of thought based on
this method of enquiry. He was struck especially by the
way that the physical world seemed to be underpinned

by relationships between pure numbers. Nature, apparently, had a mathematical infrastructure. At the same time, Pythagoras pointed out that mathematical entities are somehow subtler than their counterparts in the "real" world of the senses. A circle drawn in the sand may seem from a distance to be exactly circular but, on closer inspection, always turns out to have little bumps and dimples. A mathematical circle, on the other hand, is perfect in every way and can therefore only be pictured in the mind. From this line of thinking stemmed the theory of ideas (*idea* is Greek for "picture"), or Forms, which was developed by Socrates, Plato and others.

Pythagoras was both a mathematician and an incurable mystic. Among his many discoveries, he found that harmonious notes on a vibrating string always occur at lengths that are in simple numerical ratios to the fundamental (that is, the note made by the open vibrating string). To others this may have seemed a mere curiosity, a pleasing coincidence of nature. But to Pythagoras it was the expression of a deep mystical truth. From it, he concluded that the soul was an attunement of the body. A properly balanced body will carry a harmonious soul, just as a properly tuned string will emit a harmonious sound.

Socrates (c. 470–399 B.C.) took a different line. His theory of the soul had its roots in an earlier Pythagorean doctrine that there are three ways of life. This was exemplified by the three kinds of men who attended the Pythian games at Delphi: the athletes, the spectators and those who bought and sold. By analogy, Socrates argued that the soul has, in descending order, a rational part, an emotional part and an acquisitive part. In the just soul these are properly ordered, each minding its own business and obeying the parts ranked above. Reason, at the top, rules emotion. Emotion, in turn, helps to inspire the actions that reason dictates.

Because the just soul is ruled by reason, Socrates linked it to the realm of Forms. A Form was held to be a perfect, unchanging counterpart of something real. Socrates taught that a "particular," for example a cup, is what it is by virtue of participating in the Form, or picture, of the cup—the constant and unique prototype of cups that exists in the realm of ideas. The point is echoed in the way we use language: there are many cups of many shapes, sizes, textures and colors, but there is only one word *cup,* which we use to refer to them all. Though a cup might break, the Form remains intact, as does the word.

The realm of Forms was believed to have a definite structure and hierarchy. At the top was the Form of the Good, under which all other Forms were arranged. From this, Socrates deduced that the knowledgeable soul is bound to be good; its existence will consist in contemplating the Form of the Good. Evil, therefore, springs from ignorance, which arises when the soul is ruled by the body. Since the good soul is connected to the Forms, whereas the body belongs to the world of particulars, the soul lasts but the body does not.

Unfortunately, Socrates' conjectures about the na-

ture of the soul scarcely outlived the man himself—
thanks to Plato. Having originally championed the
theory of Forms, Plato (c. 427–347 B.C.) went on to
demolish it completely in a dialogue called the Parmenides. The setting is a meeting between the philosophers Socrates, Parmenides, and Zeno, in Athens, in
about 450 B.C. By then, Parmenides, one of the fathers
of Greek philosophy, was an old man, his disciple Zeno
was at the height of his powers, and Socrates was young
and (conveniently for Plato) still somewhat inexperi-
enced. In the dialogue, Parmenides points out that the
Forms fail to account for what we see because there is
no way of linking them with particulars. The link would
have to be either another Form or another particular,
and therefore would itself have to be linked, and so on
forever without resolution.

Having thus logically disposed of Forms, Plato went
on to develop his idea of the soul as a prime mover. In
other words, the soul is what produces motion, both of
itself and of other objects. Since this happens only in
living things, it must be their basic principle, so that
the soul comes before the body and the feelings of the
soul before the material qualities of the body. Ethical
qualities—those that determine conduct—therefore
spring from the soul. This holds not only for positive
ethical qualities but also for their opposites; evil, as
much as good, has its origins in the soul.

With Aristotle (384–322 B.C.) the basis for specu-
lation at last shifted away from pure theory to biological observation. Aristotle was not exactly a scientist in

the modern sense because he never went to the trouble of testing his ideas by experiment. But he was undoubtedly a great observer and encyclopedist. From his studies of fauna and flora he, like Socrates, saw the need for three different types of soul—in his case known as the nutritive, the sensitive and the rational. All living things require nourishment, so plants, animals and men alike must have a nutritive soul. Animals and men have both nutritive and sensitive functions. But man alone is rational. The Aristotlean relation between body and soul is the same as that between matter and form. The soul makes a man what he is but has no existence independent of the body. It is like a hallmark stamped on a bar of metal. When the body disintegrates, so does the soul. Only the rational function is not completely lost. It goes back to where it came from—a kind of reservoir of rationality, a common sea of intellectual consciousness.

Personal gods find no special place in the philosophies of Pythagoras, Socrates, Plato and Aristotle. Yet there are clear implications for morality. Socrates considered that a good life was one spent in the pursuit of the Form of the Good. For Aristotle, goodness was directly linked with the proper and consistent use of reason—always choosing the appropriate middle ground between extremes of action. The good soul is balanced, harmonious and, above all, rational.

Strange as it may seem now, the great thinkers of the Golden Age in Greece had very confused views about the role of the brain. Aristotle, the most influential of them all, never considered the brain to be a possible seat of the soul or of the mind. He believed it was just a cooling system, filled with phlegm—the mucus of a runny nose offering proof. Thought, intellect and the soul, he maintained, resided in the heart—a belief we still whimsically recall today with our "heartfelt" emotions and, symbolically, with a heart-shaped love sign. (The Egyptians also held this view, which is why they discarded the brain yet preserved or substituted the heart so that it could be weighed before Osiris on the judgment scales.)

It was only in the second century A.D. that the Greek-born physician Galen (c. 130–200 A.D.) pointed indisputably to the brain as the site of mental activity. Galen, who rose to fame after his successful treatment of the Roman emperor Marcus Aurelius, would publicly dissect the nerves in the neck of a live pig. As these were severed, one by one, the pig would continue to squeal; however, when Galen cut one of the laryngeal nerves (now also known as "Galen's nerves"), the squealing abruptly stopped, to the awe of the crowd. In this gruesome manner, Galen showed beyond doubt that it was the brain, via a network of nerves, that was in charge of the rest of the body.

Although disagreeing with Aristotle on the role of the brain, Galen did accept Aristotle's theory of the tripartite soul—indeed, he embellished it. To the three basic elements, he added imagination and memory, as well as all motor and sensory functions. Later, the

Roman Catholic Church appropriated Galen's ideas (along with many other off-the-shelf classical views about the universe), even going so far as to suggest specific sites in the brain where the various functions of the soul might reside. And there the matter lay. For more than a thousand years, no one cared to hazard an alternative theory, such was the all-pervasive and intimidating power of the Church in Europe.

Then came the Renaissance and, with it, the renewal of the spirit of enquiry. Giordano Bruno, an outspoken Dominican monk, was burned at the stake. Galileo was threatened with torture. But the tidal wave of new ideas was unstoppable and soon the Church was forced to abandon its long-held grip on the material cosmos.

Galileo himself staked out the future territory for science in 1623. Science, he asserted, was concerned only with "primary" qualities, in other words, those aspects of the external world that can be weighed and measured. "Secondary" qualities, such as beauty, love, meaning and value, were by implication of lesser importance and could be left in the hands of the artist and the theologian.

Frenchman René Descartes (1596–1650) expressed a similar sentiment. There were, he said, two radically different kinds of stuff in the universe. The first, consisting of physical, or extended, substance (*res extensa*), has length, breadth and depth, and can therefore be measured and divided. The second, or purely mental substance (*res cogitans*), is both intangible and indivisible. The outside world, including the human body, belongs to the first category, while the internal world of the mind belongs to the second.

These new, clear-cut distinctions between primary and secondary qualities, matter and mind, objective and subjective, had the effect of excluding human consciousness from the scientific picture of the world. As the historian E. A. Burtt has remarked, in the eyes of post-Renaissance science, "man was hardly more than a bundle of secondary qualities" and "not a subject suitable to mathematical study."

Insofar as man was now anything at all, he was a biological machine. The only remaining point to debate was whether, connected in some way with this flesh-and-blood machine, there was an immaterial spirit or soul.

Descartes had very definite ideas about this. Having received the best education his time could offer, Descartes rejected most of the Scholastic dogma served up by his Jesuit teachers and set out to rebuild knowledge on what he considered a firmer basis. His efforts led him to become one of the recognized founders of modern philosophy.

In the synopsis of his *Meditations on First Philosophy,* published in 1641, Descartes wrote: "What I have said is sufficient to show clearly enough that the extinction of the mind does not follow from the corruption of the body, and also to give men the hope of another life after death."

In order to reach this bold conclusion, Descartes had spent many hours in seclusion—simply thinking (a habit he acquired as a child since frail health allowed him to stay in bed on many school mornings). He thought of what he could, and could not, be positively sure about. He could not possibly doubt that he was thinking, and therefore that he was. *Cogito, ergo sum* (''I think, therefore I am''): that simple, memorable phrase has come down to us as the philosophical equivalent of Newton's laws of motion, the seemingly secure springboard for further conjecture. Even an omnipotent deceiver could not have deluded Descartes about his own existence. But such a deceiver, he realized, if sufficiently malicious, could well have deluded him about everything else! There was nothing in the indubitable fact of his thinking to guarantee that a world existed out there or that he even had a body (a sentiment that finds a curious echo in the modern quantum mechanical view of the world). The only safe conclusion was that he was a purely mental being, and that his mind was completely distinct from his body. This being so, then his mind ought to be able to continue to exist independently after his body was dead and buried. Hence, man had a soul.

It hardly seems like a revolutionary idea. After all, Descartes's ''dualism,'' or theory of two substances, has some obvious features in common with the Church's traditional view of the body and the soul. But Descartes broke sharply with religious orthodoxy in at least one very important respect—his belief that logic could unlock the secrets of the soul.

Philosophers of all persuasions now joined in the debate, unfettered (if not entirely uninfluenced) by the teachings of the Church. Do we, as Descartes maintained, have a soul that is distinct and separate from the brain? If so, then corporeal death may not be the end but simply a phase transition, a metamorphic event in which we break free of materiality as a prelude to moving on. Or, are the soul and the mind truly ephemeral—artifacts of the living brain, doomed to die when the brain dies?

One of the dualist's main problems is to come up with a mechanism—any mechanism—by which the soul and the brain can interact. This is like Plato's dilemma in trying to link Forms with particulars. It is the actual coupling that is the tricky aspect. If the soul is immaterial and the brain is made of ordinary matter, then how can the two possibly establish contact and influence each other?

Descartes had an ingenious answer to this. He accepted the earlier discovery by William Harvey, physician to Elizabeth the First, about the circulation of blood but rejected Harvey's idea that the heart was a pump. Instead he went along with Aristotle's belief that the heart was like a hearth where the blood was heated. This heating produced a vapor (the so-called "animal spirits") that dilated the brain and put it in a state ready to receive impressions from the senses and the soul. For his organ of interaction—the physical seat of the soul—Descartes chose the pineal gland. This tiny structure, he concluded, was ideally placed (at the base of the skull) to be able to regulate the flow of vapor to and from the brain.

Descartes may have been wrong about the pineal gland, but he opened the floodgates to rational debate on the subject of the soul. The English philosopher John Locke (1632–1704) pondered long and hard over the dualism issue and was not convinced by Descartes's explanation of how the soul and the brain communicate. Perhaps, he argued, mind is material and God endows matter, in man's case, with the power to think and know.

Locke remained a dualist—just. But not so his compatriot Thomas Hobbes (1588–1679). Hobbes was an out-and-out determinist, a man who had been powerfully influenced in his youth by the new "mechanical philosophy" of Galileo. All things to Hobbes could be explained as if they were machines. To him, the soul was no more than the thinking body. It is a sentiment that has been echoed many times since, most memorably in 1949 by the English philosopher Gilbert Ryle, who derided Descartes's notion of the mind as a "ghost in the machine."

Has that ghost finally been exorcised by scientific reductionism? Among the ranks of biologists and philosophers today, there is no doubt that materialists hold sway. The brain is under the microscope as never before, and the hope of many researchers seems to be that all of its functions—all that our minds are capable of—will someday be understandable in purely physical terms.

And yet, the voice of the dissidents is insistent and perhaps, once again, becoming hard to ignore. As Lewis Thomas, the distinguished cancer research administrator and writer, eloquently put it:

There is still that permanent vanishing of consciousness to be accounted for. Are we to be
stuck forever with this problem? Where on Earth
does it go? Is it simply stopped dead in its tracks,
lost in humus, wasted? Considering the tendency
of nature to find uses for complex and intricate
mechanisms, this seems to me unnatural. I prefer
to think of it somehow as separated off at the
filaments of its attachment, and then drawn like
an easy breath back into the membrane of its
origin, a fresh memory for a biospherical nervous
system . . .

The great question remains, after millennia of debate: can mind survive in some form without its neural
hardware—and, if so, in what form? Is mind just our
subjective experience of the brain at work or do mind
and brain have a separate, parallel existence?

VISIONS OF PARADISE

"The boundaries between Life and Death are at best shadowy and vague. Who shall say where one ends, and where the other begins?"

—*Edgar Allan Poe*

*I*n death, science is pitted against the equivalent of the astronomer's black hole: an impenetrable information barrier. A black hole is encircled by an "event horizon," a boundary beyond which the speed needed to escape from the black hole is greater than the speed of light—the fastest that any material object can travel. When we die, each of us makes a solo flight across the event horizon of death and gives up in that final, involuntary act all possibility of sending back news of what we find.

Or do we? Claims to the contrary, that contact can

be established with those beyond the grave, have been made on and off for many years, most forcefully by the Victorian spiritualists. Volumes have been written on the exploits of those early mediums, who insisted they were in touch with the spirit world. But sadly there is no credible evidence to back them up. On the contrary, the field of the paranormal, and of spiritualism in particular, is littered with the names of scientists who have been duped or beguiled by professional illusionists.

One of the first to succumb was Sir William Crookes, a brilliant and innovative chemist and physicist. In the early 1870s, long before he became president of the Royal Society, Crookes conducted experiments with the famous medium Daniel Dunglas Homes and attested to the veracity of a ghost called Katie King materialized by the young and attractive medium Miss Florence Cook. His involvement lent respectability and weight to the early spiritualist movement. But, in fact, Crookes was not the impartial observer that appearance suggested. Almost certainly he was Florence Cook's lover and, being married with a large family, was in no position to destroy her reputation even had he wished to do so.

By the turn of the last century, spiritualism had been largely discredited. Medium after medium confessed or was exposed as fraudulent, and sober minds must have begun to wonder how so many people had been taken in by the paraphernalia of the séance, with its conveniently darkened rooms and absurd manifestations. The

English biologist Thomas Huxley scoffed: "The only good that I can see in the demonstration of the truth of 'spiritualism' is to furnish an additional argument against suicide. Better live a crossing-sweeper here than die and be made to talk twaddle by a 'medium,' hired at a guinea a séance!"

Few things change, and even today—especially today—we are not immune to far-out claims by those ready to profit from our gullibility. Pyramidology, ancient astronauts, the Bermuda triangle, flying saucers and the rest are all hugely popular with those seeking escape from the banalities of the workaday world. The message is clear: if we want to believe in something badly enough, imagination will fill in the blanks and make even the flimsiest of accounts, the most dubious of evidence, seem plausible.

Who knows? Perhaps there is a kernel of truth in some of the phenomena that today might come under the loose headings of fringe science or the paranormal. Ghosts, poltergeists, telepathy and such may eventually be found to have some basis in reality. But we are wasting our time in building theories of what they may be or how they may fit into a wider scheme of nature until the evidence is more compelling.

Death seems to be truly like a black hole. Once across the threshold we are forever out of touch with the universe to which we belonged.

And yet, there may conceivably be a way around this news censorship. At least in principle, we could send spacecraft on data-gathering missions to within a hair's breadth of the black hole's event horizon without actually passing over. In a similar way, individuals who come near to death but then unexpectedly survive give us an opportunity to study at close range the boundary between life and what may lie beyond. They effectively serve as human sample-return probes to the mysterious frontier between this world and the next.

By good fortune, aided in recent years by improved resuscitation techniques, people do occasionally come very close to death before going on to make a spectacular and complete recovery. It may be that for periods lasting from a few seconds up to extreme cases of an hour or more, their breathing and pulse stop and they show no trace whatsoever of being conscious. They may even have been diagnosed and pronounced clinically dead. Yet, in many cases, having revived, near-death patients report having had a most remarkable experience *during the very time when their vital signs were undetectable.* Despite all outward appearances, they recollect being totally aware of everything happening around them. Moreover, they tell of having made a most extraordinary journey—floating above their body, traveling along a tunnel, reviewing their past life, and encountering a benign intelligence. For many, indeed, the near-death experience stands as the most powerful and convincing testimony yet for the existence of an afterlife.

Unusual experiences close to death have been reported on and off throughout history. Saint Paul wrote of the occasion when he felt himself snatched up into "third heaven": "Whether it was in the body, or out of the body I know not: God knoweth."

The nineteenth-century explorer David Livingstone also recalled a near-fatal encounter:

Starting and looking half round, I saw the lion just in the act of springing upon me . . . He caught my shoulder as he sprang, and we both came to the ground . . . The shock produced a stupor similar to that which seems to be felt by a mouse after the first shake of the cat. It caused a sort of dreaminess, in which there was no sense of pain nor feeling of terror, though I was quite conscious of all that was happening . . . This singular condition was not the result of any mental process . . . [It] is probably produced in all animals killed by carnivora; and, if so, is a merciful provision by our benevolent Creator for lessening the pain of death.

The concept of an almost universally peaceful end to life, even under traumatic conditions, was perhaps less well appreciated in the past than it is now. Before the advent of modern resuscitation methods, fewer people returned from the shadowy transition zone between life and death, and probably only a small fraction of those that did went on to voice their experiences. It would have been difficult to fit any sort of pattern to such sporadic accounts. Doom-mongers, of which there were plenty, could still warn solemnly of the impending "agony of death" despite counterclaims by some experienced physician-surgeons, such as Sir William Osler (1849–1919), that this was nonsense.

But today there is nothing unusual in patients being revived following cardiac arrest—the so-called Lazarus syndrome. Those who can recollect part or all of the time when their heart was stopped recall no sensation of pain, fear or anguish. On the contrary, their overwhelming impression is one of total quietude. As Livingstone suggested more than a century ago, it seems that man (and probably other higher animals) is equipped to shut off unnecessary distress close to death. Apparently, we do have a kind of physiological switch that, when thrown, allows us to carry on to the end in a haze of tranquility. In particular, the release into the brain of natural opiates called endorphins is known to block the experience of pain. But this being so, if we are equipped with a mechanism to make death easier, then how did it come about?

Evolution is not compassionate. It operates under no obligation to make life more comfortable just for our convenience. Simply, it nurtures the development of those characteristics that, from the outset, serve to improve an individual's chances of surviving long enough to breed. There can be no survival benefit whatsoever in a mechanism whose sole function is to make death easier to bear. From an evolutionary standpoint, a dying individual is irrelevant, the fate of his genes already sealed. Yet not so irrelevant is the ability of individuals to cope with, and thereby survive, extreme pain or injury *during the normal course of life.* And here we begin to see a possible origin for our near-death ameliorative.

Pain is the body's way of telling the brain that something is wrong, that corrective action is needed—fast. But too much pain is itself harmful. If part of the body is very badly damaged, then it may be counterproductive to keep on flooding the brain with pain signals. Far better, surely, to disconnect the pain and allow an already overloaded system the chance to recover in peace. Given that such a safety cutoff mechanism has evolved, it could well be that it is evoked, *as a matter of course,* during the final and irrevocable breakdown of the organism close to death. The autonomic systems of the body do not actually "know" they are dying; they merely react to severe internal disruption in the only way they can—by shutting off all tactile signals to the brain.

So, we can readily put together a working hypothesis of why the process of dying should seem generally peaceful, and even pleasant. Other aspects of the near-death experience, though, are not so easily resolved. How can it be, for instance, that patients who outwardly appear deeply unconscious, who may even have been pronounced dead by a qualified physician, are able to see and hear every event happening around them? How is it that such people can apparently be aware of their surroundings, not from the familiar vantage point of their bodies, but from an elevated view, outside themselves? And how can we account for the other, still more extraordinary experiences associated with the near-death state—the tunnel, the being of light, and so on? Such experiences are not rare, nor are they exclusively a modern phenomenon. Yet it is only within the past two decades or so that they have attracted serious scientific attention.

The spotlight of science, and the awareness of society in general, was first turned on near-death experiences by a psychiatrist from Georgia, Raymond Moody. In his bestselling book *Life After Life,* originally published in 1975, Moody presented extracts from more than a hundred cases of patients who had recovered after having been pronounced dead. These reports seemed to show that there is a remarkably consistent core of elements to the near-death experience. Moreover, unbeknownst to Moody before the publication of his book, two other investigators had been engaged in similar work and had come to virtually the same conclusions. They were Ralph Noyes, a psychiatrist at the University of Iowa College of Medicine, and Elisabeth Kübler-Ross, a leading pioneer in psychiatric theory relating to dying patients.

Noyes had been steadily accumulating case histories over a number of years. After analyzing them, he resolved that there were three main stages to the near-death experience. The first, exemplified by a struggle for survival, he called "resistance." This was followed by "review"—an episode, often accompanied by an out-of-body sensation, during which the victim saw incidents from his personal past. Stage three, or "transcendence," involved a hard-to-describe feeling of oneness with everything, combined with that of moving toward some unknown destination.

In 1972, Noyes suggested that a better understanding of this final mystical experience might help physicians in dealing with terminally ill patients. It might, as it were, take the sting out of death by offering some credible evidence of a life to come. Kübler-Ross subsequently threw her support behind this idea, pointing out that she had heard many similar accounts of NDE's from her own patients. As early as 1968, she claimed, she had become aware of the phenomenon but was reluctant to talk about it for fear of ridicule.

Drawing together these early findings of Moody, Noyes, Kübler-Ross and others, it was possible to see within the overall near-death experience a number of recurrent themes. While not all these themes occur together in every instance, they do seem to crop up time and again within any given sample of subjects. A typical "full-blown" NDE might run something like this:

A patient has just been rushed into the emergency room of a hospital having suffered a massive heart attack. She is aware of herself lying on a table, surrounded by medical staff and various life-support equipment. She feels acute and rising discomfort. At the moment of greatest physical distress, she hears herself pronounced dead. Immediately, all pain and fear disappear and are replaced by an extraordinary sense of peace and well-being. The patient is surprised to find herself apparently floating several feet above her own lifeless body. In this detached state, she is able to watch and listen with unusual clarity to the medical team at work. Later, she will be able to recall every detail of the resuscitation procedures and the conversation between her attendants. She will be able to describe details of the intravenous injection of drugs, the heart massage and the use of a defibrillator, even though she was not previously familiar with these techniques.

A new sensation takes over. The subject feels as if she is moving along a dark tunnel. Ahead, at the end of the tunnel, is a white light. This grows increasingly bright, until it is indescribably brilliant though somehow not blinding. Gradually, the light resolves itself into a humanoid shape and the subject is overwhelmed by the love and benevolence that this being of light seems to radiate. In some nonverbal way, the being communicates with the subject and asks her, in effect, whether her life has been well spent. There then follows a rapid review of the subject's life, in which the more important events appear as if projected onto a panoramic screen. Although extraordinarily detailed and comprehensive, the whole review seems to take only a few seconds.

By this stage, the subject is reluctant to give up her newfound state of peace and serenity. So content is she that she does not want to go back. However, at the last moment, she encounters a barrier beyond which she feels certain there could be no reprieve. The being of light indicates that she must return, and with that the subject is abruptly jolted back into her own body.

Inspired by Moody's accounts, Kenneth Ring, a psychologist at the University of Connecticut, was encouraged to check the findings through research of his own. After interviewing 102 people who through accident, illness or attempted suicide had come close to death, he published his results in the book *Life at Death: A Scientific Investigation of the Near-Death Experience,* published in 1980. Just over half of his subjects recounted experiences that matched some or all of the aspects of a classic full-blown NDE. Ring went on to identify five key elements of the NDE, which, he found, tended to occur in the same order. These were: a feeling of peace, an out-of-body sensation, the tunnel, the light and penetration of the light. Each successive stage was less frequently reported than the one before: peace (60 percent), out-of-body (37 percent), tunnel (23 percent), light (16 percent) and penetration of the light (10 percent). Ring's findings confirmed and, in a sense, legitimized Moody's earlier work.

In 1982, a Gallup poll suggested that 8 million adult Americans, or roughly one in twenty, had gone through a near-death experience. Of those interviewed, fully half who had at some point been near death reported having had an NDE. For the purposes of the poll, the experience was broken down into ten (not necessarily consecutive) elements, with the following results:

peace (32 percent), life review (32 percent), entering another world (32 percent), out-of-body (26 percent), accurate visual perception (23 percent), encountering other beings (23 percent), audible sounds of voices (17 percent), light (14 percent), tunnel (9 percent) and subsequent incidences of precognition (6 percent). The Gallup poll figures were not in close agreement with Ring's, but that is not surprising. In such a subjective area as this, wide statistical variations are to be expected.

Since the Gallup poll was conducted, more and more people have become interested in NDE's, until today there is a large number of societies, journals and self-help groups devoted to them. The growing body of evidence seems to rule out the possibility of mistake or hoax. Even so, a certain amount of skepticism is healthy. When such large numbers of people (including respected scientists) have already been taken in by hysteria over spiritualism and, more recently, by flying saucers, the "Geller effect," ancient astronauts and crop circles, it pays to be constantly on our intellectual guard. Millions can be wrong. Millions can be persuaded by media hype and self-proclaimed experts that something is genuine when, in fact, it is merely wishful thinking.

Yet, in the case of NDE's, it would be churlish to deny that there is real substance to the claims. Too many people, most of whom have nothing to gain from sensationalism, are involved. Too many people have apparently undergone profound personal transformations as a result of NDE's for the phenomenon simply to be dismissed out of hand.

A study of 344 NDE patients by Peter Fenwick, an eminent neuropsychiatrist at the Maudsley Hospital in London, showed that no fewer than 86 percent felt that their experience had made them more religious. Following an NDE, most people claim to be less materialistic, more grateful for life and more concerned with the welfare of others. Melvin Morse, a professor of pediatrics at the University of Washington, has focused especially on near-death experiences of children. He comments that NDE patients "have a zest for living which is hard to describe." Similarly, Kenneth Ring has found that "As a result of their experience they often exhibit a joie de vivre, a greater feeling of self-worth and a more compassionate concern for others. . . . They frequently develop a strong belief in God—even the atheists can identify with the light—but they tend to move away from the mainstream churches and to see truth in all religions."

What, then, are we to make of the NDE? Taking the phenomenon as a whole, it is as if there were some predetermined sequence of events waiting to unfold the closer a person comes to death. The great question is, do these events signify a genuine afterlife or are they somehow projections of the dying brain?

GATEWAY TO THE INFINITE

"Now I am about to take my last voyage, a great leap
into the dark."

—*Thomas Hobbes, dying*

*T*here can be no one who doesn't hope the near-
death experience is a true prelude to a blissful afterlife.
But when so much is at stake, it is surely right to
question whether what may feel so overwhelmingly
like a spiritual transformation is not in fact a very
powerful illusion conjured up by the brain as it dies.
We are not being cynical or insensitive if we ask: Are
there any theories that can adequately account for the
NDE in a nonspiritual way?

One of the more imaginative attempts to come to
grips with the NDE problem has been that of astron-

omer Carl Sagan. In his popular collection of essays, *Broca's Brain,* he wrote:

> The only alternative, so far as I can see, is that every human being, without exception, has already shared an experience like that of those travelers who return from the land of death: the sensation of flight, the emergence from darkness into light; an experience in which, at least sometimes, a heroic figure can be dimly perceived, bathed in radiance and glory. There is only one common experience that matches this description. It is called birth.

The tunnel, Sagan submits, is really a dim memory of the birth canal; the tunnel experience and the out-of-body experience are a reliving of one's birth; and the Christlike figure bathed in light at the end is none other than the surgeon who draws us into the bright, postamniotic world. At first sight, these do seem to be striking parallels. But critics have exposed serious flaws in Sagan's thesis. The birth canal would not really appear like the tunnel described in NDE's, even if the fetus were looking forward and open-eyed into it— which it is not (its eyes are closed and its face is pressed against the wall of the uterus). Moreover, the passage through the canal could hardly be construed as being pleasant or peaceful. Considering that the fetus is rudely expelled from the warm security of the womb, is squeezed and squashed unmercifully for several hours, and finally has its skull bent out of shape as it is exuded like toothpaste down the canal, the birth experience is surely the very antithesis of tranquility. Nor is the obstetrician—the individual who hauls us out kicking and spluttering into a harsh new world—likely to be remembered in our final thoughts with fondness and goodwill!

More seriously, Sagan's theory seems to demand far too much of the cognitive capacities of the unborn child. These are not such that it would remember the birth experience in a way that would make sense to an adult many years later. Much has been made in recent years of so-called age-regression under hypnosis, which purports to show that subjects can recall incidents from around the time of their own birth and even prenatally. However, more carefully controlled studies have not been able to back up this claim. They suggest instead that, without realizing it, regressed patients simply make up experiences that seem superficially plausible.

Having said this, Sagan's theory, like any good scientific theory, leaves itself open to testing. As Sagan himself pointed out, if the tunnel and out-of-body experiences are a rerun of birth, then there is one group of people who should never have them: those born by cesarean section. This straightforward test has now been done. Susan Blackmore, an experimental psychologist at the West of England University at Bristol, invited 254 people, of whom thirty-six had been born by cesarean, to fill out a questionnaire. The results seem to demolish Sagan's fascinating conjecture: both groups reported the same proportion of out-of-body and tunnel experiences.

An alternative explanation, favored by Blackmore

and probably the majority of qualified scientists working in this field, is that NDE's may be a particularly vivid form of hallucination. The origin of this theory can be traced back to the University of Chicago in 1926, where Heinrich Kluver had embarked upon a series of investigations with the hallucinogenic alkaloid mescaline. Derived from the peyote cactus, this drug has long been used among native Mexican Indian groups such as the Huichols as a purported aid to spiritual enlightenment. Kluver's special interest, shared by a number of other researchers in Germany and the United States at this time, was the mental imagery induced by such hallucinogens. To this end, he experimented with the drug himself.

What Kluver found, and has since been confirmed, is that among the types of false perception brought about by mescaline are four relatively simple recurrent patterns. These are the honeycomb or lattice, the cobweb, the spiral and—a familiar structure—the tunnel.

Kluver went on to observe that these four form constants, the standard motifs of drug-induced imagery, were not just confined to mescaline or even to other hallucinogens such as tetrahydrocannabinol (the active principle in marijuana and hashish) and lysergic acid diethylamide (LSD). They cropped up again and again in a wide range of hallucinatory conditions, the list of which has been extended by other investigators to include epilepsy, migraine, psychotic episodes, advanced syphilis, sensory deprivation, oxygen deprivation, insulin hypoglycemia, falling asleep, waking, meditating and applying pressure to both eyes.

Is the tunnel so often reported by those who have come close to death none other than that seen by the peyote user or the migraine sufferer? But then, what of the bright light in the center of the field of vision—the light at the end of the tunnel? This, too, it turns out, is a common enough feature of hallucinations induced by drugs and abnormal physical and mental states.

To understand how these hallucinations may come about we need to focus on that part of the brain in which mental images are formed. The visual cortex, located toward the back of the brain, handles both vision and visual imagination. In other words, it is capable of putting together pictures either from direct sensory input or from memory. Normally, the information arriving directly from the optic nerves takes precedence over internally generated imagery. What happens is that the neurons carrying the "real time" input of new data from the outside world inhibit other neurons from bringing previous perceptions and stored information to our attention. This is the normal or stable state of the visual cortex. During hallucination, however, the inhibitory mechanism is blocked, leading to an unstable and excited state.

To appreciate more clearly what happens, imagine a man standing at a closed window opposite his fireplace and looking out at the sunset. So absorbed is he by the view of the outside world that he fails to notice the weakly mirrored interior of the room. But as darkness falls outside, the images of the objects in the room behind him can be seen dimly reflected in the window. As darkness grows, the fire in the fireplace provides the main source of illumination, and the man now sees a vivid reflection of the room, *which seems to be outside the window*. The daylight (the sensory input) is reduced, while the interior illumination (the general level of arousal of the central nervous system) remains at a constant brightness. Because of this, images originating within the room (the brain) are perceived as if they came from outside the window (the senses).

Hallucinations occur, then, when some blocking agent interferes with the normal influx of sensory data. The hallucinations themselves are always there, like background noise in our mind. But we become aware of them only when the intensity of external images (and of the normal, memory-stimulated images of dreams and daydreams) is turned down.

Given the rich variety of possible hallucinogenic conditions, it seems at first surprising that hallucination should give rise to such a narrow range of basic visual forms. Why, for instance, the tunnel? What processes within the brain could generate such a structure? And, more to the point, how might its generation take place in a brain that is on the brink of death?

In 1982, Jack Cowan, a neurobiologist at the University of Chicago, furnished a valuable clue. Drawing an analogy from the way fluids behave, he argued that any sudden increase in cortical excitability would disrupt the brain's normal state and cause "stripes" of activity to travel across the visual cortex. These stripes would be like the crests and troughs of ripples that spread out from a disturbance on the surface of a pond.

What kind of mental imagery, Cowan asked, would such stripes give rise to?

Everything we see is represented first as a pattern of sensory rod and cone cells in the retina and then as a faithful copy of that pattern in different parts of the visual cortex. The entire picture is mapped from retina to brain by a complex mathematical function. Cowan showed that because of the nature of this function, *stripes of activity in the excited cortex would be perceived as though they were concentric rings, tunnels or spirals in the world outside.* Movement of the stripes would produce expansion or shrinking. Furthermore, because a much higher concentration of neurons is devoted to the center of the field of vision than to the periphery, a much greater effect could be expected in the center (assuming that all neurons were equally affected by the release from inhibition). This provides a natural explanation not only for the tunnel but for the brilliant light at the tunnel's end. The crucial question remains: Is the near-death experience simply a hallucination?

One of the greatest challenges to the hallucination theory is to explain why NDE's seem so remarkably real—far more real than the false imagery known to be generated, for example, by drugs or by oxygen deprivation. Many people are persuaded during NDE's that the tunnel is a physical connection between this world and the next. The out-of-body sensation leaves them convinced that their spirit has fled their body and can sense and move around without it. The flood of positive emotion is so intense that many are genuinely upset and angry at having to return. Why do these experiences generate such powerfully realistic impressions?

As the American psychologist and philosopher William James pointed out: "What we perceive comes as much from inside our heads as from outside." We take for granted that whatever we see and hear in our minds, as a result of our senses, is what is really "out there." But it is not that straightforward. From the moment visual or auditory processing begins, incoming sensory data gets thoroughly mixed in with information already held in memory. This is all part of the process of making useful sense of the riot of signals that constantly bombards us. Out of the confusion, our brains extract and manufacture edges, textures, perspectives, objects, spaces and other artifacts. But, this being so, how can we know what is real? How can we tell which aspects of the image we finally see in our mind's eye came from outside and which have been constructed? The short answer is, we can never tell for sure. Nevertheless, the brain, from a survival standpoint, has to make a decision on what it *thinks* is real and what is not. A reasonable assumption is that the brain latches on to the most stable overall model of the world it has at any given time and calls that "reality." In normal life the only model in contention, the only one that has the stability, coherence and complexity to appear real, is the one built up from sensory input.

But what happens as we die? Where does the brain turn to for an acceptable model of reality when the senses start to shut down and internal noise threatens to overwhelm the higher centers of the nervous system? Maybe under these extreme conditions, the stripes of activity in the visual cortex *are* the most stable model the brain has left, so that the perception these stripes produce—of moving along a tunnel toward a bright light—inevitably appears real.

At the same time, being a superb survival machine, the brain might be expected to fight hard to stay in touch with events happening in the world outside. Some of the required information might continue to feed in through the senses, particularly the sounds of voices or those of bleeping monitors and other instruments. The powerful jolts from attempted resuscitations could supply further clues as to what was "really" going on. Using these limited sensory data as a starting point, a dying patient could flesh out the scene with images pulled from memory of, for example, a hospital emergency room (often realistically depicted on TV). And there is an interesting fact about memory models: they are often in bird's-eye view. So, we have yet another possible natural explanation for a key element of NDE's—the out-of-body experience.

If the way our memories store models really is the cause of out-of-body experiences, then people who have these experiences ought to have a better-than-average ability to imagine scenes from above. The same people might also be expected to recall and dream about things from a similar vantage point. Both these ideas have been supported in tests carried out by Susan

Blackmore at Bristol and Harvey Irwin at the University of New South Wales, Australia.

As to the detailed life review often experienced during an NDE, this too can be partially accounted for. During the course of operations in the 1950s intended to cure people with severe epilepsy, Canadian surgeon Wilder Penfield passed a gentle electric current through electrodes touching specific parts of the visual cortex. The results were startling. Patients (who were only locally anesthetized) suddenly remembered scenes and events from the past in outstanding detail. The electrical stimulation seemed to trigger not just a normal recall but an apparent reliving of the event, complete with authentic sights, sounds and smells. As soon as the current was shut off, the induced recollection was immediately lost. But it could often be resumed once more by stimulating the same area. Interestingly, the recall did not pick up where it had left off but started again at the beginning, as if it were stored on videotape that rewound itself each time it was interrupted. This suggests that a record of incidents from our life is stored subconsciously in quite remarkable detail and that it can be brought to our awareness under the right conditions of stimulation. Conceivably, the waves of cortical activity that might produce the tunnel experience might also trigger the rapid playback of our archived personal histories.

Finally, there is the meeting with other beings, including the "Being of Light," to be addressed. This is perhaps the least problematic of all the elements of the experience. Surveys of NDE subjects from different cultural backgrounds, such as those conducted by Bruce Greyson, a psychiatrist from the University of Michigan Medical Center, have revealed a marked variation in the type of encounters that take place. Those of an orthodox Christian persuasion often recognize the brilliant light source as being Jesus, although the archangel Gabriel and Saint Peter are sometimes cited. Hindus more frequently meet up with some kind of messenger, who consults a list of names. Having concluded that a wrong person has been called up, the messenger gives a reprieve. An African doctor, Nsama Mumbwe of the University of Zambia, recorded this account from an eighty-five-year-old grandmother:

"I was suffering from a stroke. During this time I felt I was put into a big calabash [an empty gourd shell] with a big opening. But somehow I couldn't get out. Then a voice from somewhere said to me, 'Be brave. Take my hand and come out. It is not yet your time to go.'

"After some time of being in the calabash I managed to get out on my own.

"I believe someone was trying to bewitch me, but found that I was an innocent soul."

Accounts like this are reminiscent of tales told to young children. And that may be exactly what they are. If the brain believes it is dying, what could be more natural than in its final moments it should call up its most firmly entrenched notion of the afterlife—the one laid down when we are most impressionable, in early childhood? Beautiful gardens, smiling people in white robes, reunion with deceased loved ones, a fatherly, all-embracing God—these are all pictures painted for us by our parents in our formative years. Even professed atheists probably have a stereotyped image of Saint Peter standing at his pearly gates tucked away somewhere in the attic of their minds. Likewise, people of other cultures and religions will encounter the beings who populate their afterlife myths.

Materialists and skeptics, then, are not dumbfounded by the near-death experience. They would argue persuasively, in fact, that a theory based on hallucinations goes a long way to explaining most of the mysteries of the NDE.

Critics of this theory hark back to the superrealism of the NDE, which sets it apart from all previously known types of hallucination. They point also to the permanent, life-transforming effect of the NDE, which is often akin to a religious conversion. These arguments, though, are not entirely convincing. A person near death is in the most extreme condition imaginable, so that *any* perceptions received at that time—hallucinatory or not—could be expected to seem extraordinarily vivid and memorable. This, combined with the subconscious anticipation of some kind of momentous, final event, which probably most of us have had hard-wired into our brains from early childhood, could well be enough to produce an overwhelming and permanent impression.

The hallucination theory, moreover, draws upon only what we already know to be true, or can easily surmise, about the way the brain works. A general guiding principle in science, known as Occam's razor, is that new concepts should not be brought in unnecessarily: all things being equal, the preferable of two theories is the simpler. Why go out of our way to speculate that NDE's offer proof of life after death if we already have in our grasp a good working explanation based on more commonplace phenomena?

Frankly, it is very easy to persuade large numbers of people, through emotive anecdotal tales, that the afterlife theory is right—because that is what everyone wants to believe. But we run the risk of being crushingly disappointed (as the believers in spiritualism were) if we place too much personal stock in the afterlife interpretation of NDE's and then find this is undermined by future research.

Yet the idea that NDE's are mere concoctions of the dying brain is far from being home and dry. Two particular pieces of evidence would, if substantiated, be difficult to reconcile with the theory of hallucinations.

Among others, Michael Sabom, a cardiologist from Atlanta, has claimed that patients have seen things during NDE's that they could not possibly have reconstructed from auditory cues or from what they may previously have known about resuscitation techniques. One of the anecdotes he refers to is about a shoe seen on an inaccessible window ledge by a person while she was supposedly out of her body. Other stories tell of patients recalling the positions of needles on medical instruments and the detailed appearances of doctors and nurses during the time of the NDE. Sabom asked a group of volunteers who had never had a near-death experience to imagine going through a resuscitation procedure and to tell him what they saw in their minds. The accounts, he claims, were nothing like the accurate descriptions of apparatus or the readings on instruments that NDEers report having seen from out of the body.

The other piece of evidence that seems to cast doubt on the hallucination theory comes from instances in which an electroencephalograph, or EEG, was connected to patients during the time of their NDE. The results seem to suggest that out-of-body experiences may have happened while the EEG readings were completely flat, that is, while there was no measurable brain-wave activity of any kind. The hallucination theory requires that the brain be active in generating an NDE.

How are these remarkable claims to be addressed? First, concerning Sabom's work, there are loopholes in his experimental procedure. Since the members of his control group were not subjected to the same resuscitation procedure and actions of the staff, any comparisons drawn between them and NDE patients carry limited value.

Also, it has so far proved virtually impossible to confirm or deny any of the often-quoted stories of patients seeing things while supposedly out-of-body. Investigators such as Susan Blackmore tried, only to find that the trail had gone very cold. The patients either had since died or were confused about the exact details of their experiences, doctors and nurses were equally uncertain as to what had actually happened, and there were very few records of instrument readings or procedures carried out at the time. This is not to imply that anyone has tried to mislead, only that anecdotal tales have to be treated with the greatest caution. Many of the bestselling books about NDE's are packed with such unverifiable accounts, as if their repetition strengthens the case for an afterlife interpretation. It does not.

Formidable problems exist in collating the subjective information given by patients with reliable and accurate objective data from the scene. In the first place, no one can predict when an NDE is going to happen, and it is obviously not feasible for doctors and other staff (most of whom are dismissive of NDE's anyway) to be on constant alert for the phenomenon. The attendants' main concern, in any case, is to revive the patient, not to take notes on the circumstances of the event. And finally, after an NDE is reported to have taken place, it is impossible to tell exactly when it happened since the patient who underwent the experience had no access to a clock. In short, in the case of every NDE described to date, we have little more than second- or third-hand fireside tales and irreproducible data.

As for the EEG evidence, there is a general problem with the sensitivity of these machines, especially at low levels of brain activity. EEG's occasionally pick up spurious signals (through interference) when they are not even connected to a living brain. In one test, for instance, Jell-O gave positive readings. Conversely, there have been times when EEG's sensed no brain-wave patterns in patients who, from other vital signs, were known to be alive. The brain activity can be going on at such a deep level that electrodes on the surface of the scalp fail to pick it up. And, again, there is the difficulty of correlating the period of the flat trace with the time during which the NDE took place.

Physicians and psychologists who have written on the near-death experience make much about the tunnel, the out-of-body sensation and especially the Being of Light. These effects, as we have seen, are not impossible to explain in terms of universal processes that happen in the dying brain.

However, there is one aspect of the NDE that we have not yet dealt with but that poses an enormous problem for the materialist. It is hard for the person who feels it to describe. It seems to go beyond words. But what it apparently consists of is an extraordinary deepening and broadening of consciousness as ordinary life comes to an end. Coupled with this increase in overall consciousness is a progressive lessening of self-awareness. As the experience unfolds, the subjects, it seems, become more and more conscious of everything except themselves.

This is the core enigma of the NDE. Why should it be that as the brain dies, consciousness expands? And why should it be that as consciousness expands, self-consciousness disappears?

This much is certain: for those who have made the journey to the netherlands of life, the effect is profound. Whatever may lie behind the NDE—whether it is truly evidence of life after death or a mere artifact of the dying brain—makes no difference in one important respect. The NDE is life-transforming. For a while, at least, other worlds appear on an equal footing with our own—as real as the familiar reality we thought unique. The body is seen to be of little consequence, and for some who go through the process all sense of being an individual is lost. Indeed, the NDE reveals something quite astonishing about the human condition. It affords a disturbing peek into the artificial nature of self and the world: neither can seem so substantial again.

SELFISH THOUGHTS

"If you work on your mind with your mind, how
can you avoid an immense confusion?"

—*Seng Ts'an, Chinese philosopher*

*W*here did "you" come from? What led up to this
extravagant arrangement of stardust—yourself—that
can imagine and cast its thoughts far into the past or the
as-yet-unknowable future, that can foresee its own end
and even speculate on what may lie beyond the fron-
tiers of death?

The stuff of which we are all made traces its origin back
to the Big Bang itself. In this unique event, cosmologists believe, all the raw material the universe would
ever contain burst out of a point far smaller than the

period at the end of this sentence. It was the ultimate conjuring trick. Out of that tiny genesis seed grew the whole cosmos we see today, teeming with a hundred billion galaxies and ten billion trillion stars.

Only the two lightest elements, hydrogen and helium, were made in the immediate aftermath of the Big Bang. All the rest, up to and including iron, had to wait to be cooked deep inside the hot cores of giant stars. These big suns then blew apart spectacularly as supernovas (creating small quantities of still heavier nuclei) and hurled their remains far into space. After billions of years, some of this scattered debris, laced with all the naturally occurring heavier elements up to uranium, found its way into growing clouds of gas and dust from which new stars would eventually form—one of them, the sun.

From what was left of the dusty cloud that spun around the infant sun came the planets of the solar system. And from the atoms of one of these worlds, in time, came ourselves. No wonder we sometimes look up at the night sky and imagine our future out there, among the stars, crossing the light-years. We have made that journey before.

Yet it was here, on earth, that we first became aware of our ancestry—and our inheritance. Here life began, we believe, as unshielded far-ultraviolet rays from the sun and powerful lightning discharges set off complex reactions in the rich chemical broth of earth's primordial seas.

*   *   *

Origins fascinate us. Our minds have an incurable habit of seeking out decisive moments. When did the universe begin? When did life first appear? We are like the character in Robert Frost's poem:

> You're searching, Joe
> For things that don't exist.
> I mean beginnings
> Ends and beginnings
> Ends and beginnings—there are
> no such things
> There are only middles.

We're forever dividing up the world and labeling it. We're always on the lookout for what we think might be crises or transitions so we can claim something new has appeared—and then stick a name tag on it. And so we talk about "events" like the "origin of life." But we need to shake ourselves sometimes and remember that our labels are totally, unreservedly artificial. "Life" and "nonlife" are made-up categories like all the others we impose on the world. There are no such distinctions in reality.

Living things, as we conventionally think of them, grow, respire, take in food, put out waste. Most important, they reproduce. To be alive, we say, an organism has to be able to make faithful copies of itself, generation after generation. It seems to be a definition that works fine for zebras and honeybees and humans. But the question of what lives and what doesn't starts to get more problematic as soon as we move away from the "middles."

Take stars, for instance. They grow as they form. They ingest whatever falls onto their surface. They excrete stellar winds and flares. They even reproduce in the sense that the stuff of which they're made is recycled into new stars. So, why isn't a star alive?

Perhaps it is. If we all agreed tomorrow that stars were alive they *would be* alive. "Life" is our invention, so we can do with it as we please. We only have to make changes in our worldview by global consent for living stars to become part of our invented reality. If you grew up in a culture which taught that stars (and maybe also planets and rocks and atoms) were alive, then that's exactly what you would believe. Whatever cosmic perspective, whatever labeling system we are brought up to accept as "true" defines for us what nature is like.

But it is all a fiction. Life, death, stars, objects and events of every kind are convenient lies—received but false wisdom. What to us seem like certain facts are merely agreements between ourselves within a framework of interpretation. Change, impermanence and undividedness are the true qualities of the universe. And the sooner we get deeply acquainted with that, the sooner we can understand better what we really are and where we are heading.

Things abound in the human universe. The way our brains have evolved has made them compulsive analyzers and classifiers. We see objects everywhere. And we see boundaries everywhere, because a boundary defines the object within.

If there is a boundary, as we perceive it, then there is an individual. So we talk about an individual star or planet or rock or microbe. Why is it, though, that of these only the microbe is considered to be alive? Forget details like genes and chromosomes—we can imagine life with a different physical basis. The real reason we say the microbe is alive is that it seems to us to act purposefully. It behaves so, not in the sense that it thinks, but in the more limited sense that it *controls* what passes through the boundary between itself and the outside world. And notice that in talking about life in this way, another label has crept in—*self*.

To be a "self," as we see it, is to know what is good for you. Recognizing food, avoiding danger and knowing the difference between what is part of you and what is not are elementary skills that any aspiring life-form must have. To be alive is, in the very way we define it, to have a degree of selfhood. The "knowledge" of self may be expressed at a very low level by the physical and chemical processes that go on inside a primitive, one-celled animal. But that is knowledge enough. Long before brains and nervous systems evolved, there were organisms looking out for their own interests. Even as life began, so too did self.

And consciousness? That seems to be a much loftier property. We generally think of it as marking out humans and other "higher" animals from lesser forms of life. Even such a marvelously complex thing as a fly isn't usually considered to be in any way conscious. And yet wasn't the springboard for consciousness surely just the ability of an organism to sense some aspects of its surroundings and react in a way that improves its survival chances? Every living thing has to have this ability or it quickly dies before it can pass on its genes. Life, apparently, implies some degree of selfhood, which, in turn, implies some degree of consciousness: all three must have grown up together.

On the face of it, a microbe's "consciousness" isn't much. At best it seems to encompass a low sensitivity and inclination to react to what happens in the environment. But doesn't an electron also "sense" and "react" when struck by another particle? Couldn't we therefore say that an electron—one of the smallest particles in nature—was also vaguely conscious? And if so, doesn't this imply that every single bit of the universe is somehow aware?

A very different picture of reality begins to emerge, then, as we challenge some of the categorizations of orthodox science. In fact, there is a deeper truth beyond science, beyond any form of rationalization, that has been known to the human race for a very long time. It is an intuitive, direct form of knowledge and not one that can or needs to be proven. As Max Planck said: "Science cannot solve the ultimate mystery in Nature. And it is because in the last analysis we ourselves are part of the mystery we are trying to solve."

Fifteen hundred years earlier Buddha voiced a similar thought: "In the search for truth there are certain questions that are not important. Of what material is the universe constructed? Is the universe eternal? Are there limits or not to the universe? . . . If a man were to postpone his search for Enlightenment until such questions were solved, he would die before he found the path.''

We live our lives entirely inside an illusion—a virtual reality far more convincing than any yet created by computer. So mesmerized are we by it that we find the greatest difficulty in imagining that the world could be any other way. Everywhere we look are objects and events and phenomena, from the most trivial happenings in our everyday lives to the creation of the universe. Yet it is all a mirage, a fabulous invention. And the most extraordinary, convincing part of it is ourselves. Where exactly did "we" come from?

Life started, in the conventional view, as a happy product of molecules bumping into one another and occasionally sticking together. Eventually, inevitably perhaps, one particular group of molecules came together that had the unusual property of being able to make exact copies of itself. These copies spawned more of their kind, and so it went on. Soon, the ancient waters of earth were swarming with elementary, self-replicating "life-forms." Changes to the environment, some brought about by the new presence of life, others not, spurred the development of further types of organism. Competition began. There were survival advantages in having, among other qualities, improved senses.

So, in time, creatures emerged with primitive eyes and ears and other organs with which to better perceive their environment. Century by century, the developments were insignificantly small. But over many millions of years, through a combination of environmental pressure and random genetic variation, the growth of more advanced life-forms was encouraged. Bundles of nerve fibers organized themselves into crude biological switchboards, which in turn became the prototypes of the first rudimentary brains.

Some researchers, such as Richard Dawkins, choose to see evolution as a battle for supremacy between rival genes. Organisms, according to this view, are merely the unwitting agencies through which genes express themselves, compete with others of their kind and vie to secure their transmission to new hosts. The ''selfish gene'' paradigm offers a refreshingly novel insight into the way biological complexity and diversity may have come about. But we can look at the unfolding of nature from many different levels and perspectives.

At the far end of the scale from genes, we can see evolution as being a general, unpremeditated drift toward higher and higher levels of self-awareness. The more clearly an organism can see itself as an agent in the internal world it builds, the better are its chances of outwitting and outguessing its competitors. This is not to suggest that every creature is bent upon becoming smarter. Once a species has adapted fully to a particular niche, it doesn't evolve further unless fresh demands are placed on it. There will always be jellyfish, and they will always be stupid. Good brains are needed only by animals competing for certain types of complex, unspecialized niches—niches that opened up only after those at a more elementary level had been occupied. And yet it is these brainy creatures that, from our biased human viewpoint, appear to define evolution's leading edge.

Throughout the ascent of life on earth, "self" has become an increasingly important factor. But it is only quite recently that its development has so dramatically accelerated. By 300 million years ago, self-awareness was still at a fairly low level. The first land vertebrates, primitive reptiles, had just completed their escape from the oceans; and a reptile's brain is a meager, unversatile affair. Of the three main regions that comprise every vertebrate's brain—hindbrain, midbrain and forebrain—a reptile is endowed significantly with only the first two. In human terms, it has little more than a brain stem.

The reptile's sensory world was (and is) centered mainly on vision. But unlike our own visual system, which allows us to interpret and manipulate and conjecture about what we see, a reptile's ability to detect and process visual information is largely hard-wired into the circuitry of its eyes and its midbrain. Thus a reptile is a slave, rather than a master, of its environment—a sophisticated biological automaton.

By 200 million years ago, however, there had come a major neurological breakthrough. The first mammals had appeared, with brains four to five times bigger relative to body weight than those of their reptilian counterparts. Almost all the increase was due to the dramatic appearance of the cerebral cortex, a thin "thinking cap" of gray cells atop the forebrain that gave its owner an unprecedented new faculty for building internal world models. But why did the brain evolve so rapidly at this time?

What is clear is that the first mammals, which were nocturnal, would have been poorly served by reptilian sight. Being small and warm-blooded, they needed constantly to refuel themselves, so they scavenged for food virtually the whole time they were awake. This meant having to actively seek out insects and other elusive prey during the hours of darkness. Sight alone was not enough for them. They needed improved senses of smell and hearing and thus larger and more sophisticated olfactory and auditory systems. Evolving such systems forced in turn a radical restructuring of the nervous system. Reptiles could get by with the equivalent, in computer terms, of ROM-based handling of visual data—the hard-wired approach. But the far trickier task of extracting accurate 3-D spatial and temporal information from sounds and smells called for machinery in the brain capable of processing sensory input at a much higher level. Simply tacking on a mass of nerve cells at the periphery of the nervous system, as reptiles had done with their eyes, was out of the question; there was not enough room.

This sharp contrast with the packaging demands of the reptilian visual system was, according to Harry

Jerison of the University of California at Los Angeles, one of two main factors that prompted the growth in relative brain size of the early mammals. The second stemmed from a further benefit of having a more centralized processing system: the opportunity to integrate the sensory signals from sight, sound, smell and touch to create a more detailed and *artificial* mental picture of the world.

With their new cortices, the early mammals were far better equipped to generate their own internal reality than were the reptiles. They were more perceptive and more able to respond pliantly to the world they saw.

Once established, the mammalian brain plateaued in relative size for at least 100 million years. Then came another explosive period of growth. Following the sudden demise of the dinosaurs, about 65 million years ago, modern mammals began to evolve at prodigious speed. Over the next 30 million years their brains ballooned four- to five-fold, with the biggest gains coinciding with the appearance of the ungulates (hoofed mammals), carnivores and primates. Most of this new growth, Jerison argues, was probably due to the mammals invading daytime niches left vacant by the dinosaurs and their relatives. Having adapted to a nocturnal way of life, mammals now had to reevolve diurnal sight. As it was impossible to go back to the old reptilian arrangement, the revamped visual system had to be incorporated into the forebrain along with new connections to the nerve centers handling hearing and smell. In consequence, the cortex once again expanded enormously, and with it the capacity to fashion a still more lucid model of the world.

In one particular group of mammals, the primates, the brain-to-body-size ratio, or encephalization quotient (EQ), became especially large. For their size, monkeys and apes have brains two to three times as big as that of an average modern mammal, while a human being has an EQ roughly three times as big as a chimpanzee's. Why is it that our brains have grown so much?

There are no simple answers, but two theories are popular. Some researchers, like John Allman of the California Institute of Technology, point to a link between increased brain size and the evolution of better strategies for ensuring a stable supply of food and other resources. Man's ancestors almost certainly had to exploit a wide home base, make inventive use of whatever was locally at hand in their search for food, and broaden their diet. This, in turn, says Allman, demanded improved cognitive skills.

Robin Dunbar, professor of biological anthropology at University College, London, is among those in the rival theorists' camp. He champions complex social behavior of primates as the main driving force behind bigger brains. In 1992, he completed a survey of thirty-eight genera of primates, including gorillas, chimpanzees and humans, and found that those species dwelling in large social groups, such as chimps and baboons, boast proportionately larger cortices. Bigger primate groups, Dunbar concludes, have a need for greater social cohesion and hence more advanced skills for communicating and keeping track of group relationships. This might explain, among other things, our obsession with social tittle-tattle in the tabloid press and why gossip about relationships takes up so much of our conversation.

To find out just how important gossip is, Dunbar and his colleagues monitored conversations in a university cafeteria, scoring the topic every half-minute. Even in such a supposedly academic environment, talk about social relationships and personal experiences took up nearly 70 percent of the conversations, with half of this devoted to gossip about people not present. Males, however, tended to focus more on their own relationships and experiences, whereas females talked mostly about other people's.

Could this mean, as Dunbar has speculated, that language evolved mainly as a vehicle by which females circulated news within their group—social chitchat that was vital to the group's stability? The anthropological party line is that it grew up in the context of male-male relationships, as a means, for example, of coordinating hunting or defense. But the idea that interfemale social exchanges may have been the main spur to linguistic development ties in well with another observation—that in nonhuman-primate societies, female-female relationships are all-important. At any rate, it gives the modern male something to think about. The next time he complains about his partner's propensity for gossip, he might consider that without it he could himself have been left speechless.

Doubtless a whole raft of interwoven factors, environmental and social, helped the primate brain grow. But in the ancestors of our own species this development just went on and on. In less than 3 million years, the brain tripled in size and evolved a cortex that, in modern man, accounts for an astonishing 70 to 80 percent of brain volume.

An average human brain contains 10 billion to 15 billion neurons with up to ten times as many glial, or connecting, cells. The possible number of ways of joining all these cells together is much greater than all of the atoms in the universe. But the strange fact is, it seems as if we have a far bigger brain than we strictly need to think and behave as we do.

Cerebral size alone is no sure guide to intelligence. Some severely retarded people have larger-than-average brains, while among those of unusual brilliance brain size can vary by almost a factor of two. Not many eminent individuals, as might be expected, have had their brains weighed, but of those that have the current record holder is the Russian writer Ivan Turgenev, whose brain tipped the scales at 2,012 grams, or more than four pounds. (A typical adult male brain weighs three pounds.) By contrast, the French novelist Anatole France struggled by (winning the 1921 Nobel prize for literature) with a puny brain of just 1,017 grams (barely two pounds). Other gifted neural lightweights include Franz Gall, ironically the founder of phrenology (the study of cranial bumps), and Walt Whitman, whose poetic genius emanated from a brain of just 1,282 grams.

One might suppose there is a limit to how small a brain can be before the effects start to show. And this is generally true. So-called microcephalics have very small brains and correspondingly low intelligence. Most extreme of all are anencephalics—babies with empty skulls, who die shortly after birth.

However, the very-small-brain/very-low-intelligence rule doesn't always hold. In the mid-1960s, the world learned of (and has since largely forgotten) the remarkable case of certain hydranencephalics. The news broke in the form of a paper in the journal *Developmental Medicine and Child Neurology* by John Lorber of the University of Sheffield, England. It described two children with water not "on the brain" but *in place of* a brain. They had fluid where their cerebrums should have been. A light shone into their skulls would have revealed the disturbing phenomenon of transillumination—the rays would have passed cleanly through from one side to the other. Yet, what was so astonishing was that although neither child showed any evidence of having a cerebral cortex, the mental development of each appeared perfectly normal. One child subsequently died at three months. The other was still healthy and continuing to develop like a normal child a year later.

Lorber's paper was reported, briefly, without much fuss, in popular science magazines at the time, and then faded from view. Why? Perhaps because it raised too many problems or was too far off the beaten track of conventional brain science. In any event, the work quietly continued and other externally normal, gross hydranencephalics were found. One was a man with an IQ of 126 who had graduated from the University of Sheffield with a first-class honors degree in mathematics. He was bright, conventional in appearance and behavior, but had no detectable brain.

A pair of identical-twin girls with gross hydranencephalus were also studied. Both had above-average IQs. In another case, a young man who had suddenly died had an autopsy, which revealed only the most paltry rind of brain tissue. Trying to console his parents, the coroner expressed grief tempered by relief that such a profoundly retarded lad had finally found rest. Dumbfounded, the parents told the coroner that their son had been at work just two days before.

Intelligent hydranencephalics make nonsense of received neurological wisdom—another possible reason that they have been so conspicuously ignored. With cerebrums in some cases less than a fifth of an inch thick, they have brains smaller than that of a rabbit yet function like perfectly normal human beings. How? The only possible answer is that they are making the best use of what limited processing capacity they have. But this raises the question, if we only need brains this small, why has evolution given us brains that are so much larger? It seems that, as the British naturalist Alfred Russel Wallace pointed out, "an instrument has been developed in advance of the needs of its possessor."

Like other parts of the human body, the brain apparently includes a very high degree of redundancy. We can make do with less than 10 percent of our digestive tract, a quarter of one kidney and a snippet of liver. Now we find that the brain, too, has a massive amount of spare capacity. Its great bulk looks impressive but most of it—perhaps 90 percent or more—is a safety buffer built into the cortex over millions of years of development. That is not to say we can just lose nine-tenths of our brain and carry on as normal. Even modest damage to a major structure is enough to deprive us of sight or speech or memory. But we apparently use only a small fraction of the brain's *overall* potential. As writer Arthur Koestler remarked: "It is the only example of evolution providing a species with an organ it does not know how to use; a luxury organ, which will take its owner thousands of years to learn to put to proper use—if it ever does." An early hint, perhaps, of what the human race might someday be capable of.

Our ancestors started to look vaguely human well before they could think in a human way. Genetic and fossil evidence suggests that the first protohominids appeared somewhere between 7.5 million and 5 million years ago. Partial skeletons, 3.5 million years old, have been found of a small, lightly built creature called *Australopithecus afarensis* who clearly walked upright—he even left us footprints—but whose EQ seems to have been no bigger than that of a chimp. We were bipedal before we were brainy. A million years later, however, the cortex was once again on the move. Around this time the climate of the world started to change, becoming cooler and drier. Areas of Africa once densely forested turned to open savannah. These environmental changes triggered a complex sequence of events out of which emerged the first of our direct forebears, *Homo habilis,* or "Skillful Man."

It can be no coincidence that the earliest stone tools, global cooling and the oldest remains of *H. habilis* all date back to more or less the same period of time. Skillful Man earns his name by having been the first significant tool-user. But was he also the instigator of human language? Could habiline man utter the rudiments of a spoken tongue, or did that development take place much later?

From looking closely into fossilized crania, Dean Falk at the State University of New York, Albany, has concluded that spoken language began to develop between 2 million and 3 million years ago with the incipience of the genus *Homo.* He cites a famous 1.9-million-year-old skull found east of Lake Turkana in northern Kenya. This reveals a slight bulge on the left side near the temple corresponding to what in a modern human brain would be the location of Broca's area—a region thought to play a key role in vocalization.

Studies of the way the voice box has developed also lend credence to the idea that language emerged quite early in our evolution. Humans are unique in having a larynx low in the throat, an arrangement that leaves a bigger air space above and so extends the range of possible sounds that can be made. The position of the larynx is reflected in the shape of the underside of the skull, or basicranium. In chimps, this is relatively flat, whereas in humans it forms an arch. Unfortunately, no intact basicranium of habiline man has yet come to light. However, the remains of a 1.6-million-year-old *Homo erectus* ("Upright Man") have been found with a basicranium flexed to a position midway between that of an ape and a modern human. Since *H. erectus* stands in direct line between us and our remote habiline fore-bears, it is tempting to speculate that spoken language may have started its long, slow development at least 2 million years ago.

Others see it differently. Probably the world's fore-most linguist, Noam Chomsky, of the Massachusetts Institute of Technology, insists that natural language is unique to our particular species, *Homo sapiens*. This would bring the origins of human speech forward to no more than 250,000 years ago. His argument is based on a comparison of the brains of contemporary humans and apes. No language-related structure in the ape cortex, he maintains, bears any resemblance to the neural basis of speech in man. However, researchers such as Steven Pinker of MIT and Paul Bloom of the University of Arizona have taken issue with Chomsky on this. They point out that our closest living relatives, the African apes, have been through at least 5 million years of independent evolution since we shared a com-mon ancestor. Human language is so complex, they

insist, that both it and the neural hardware that sub-
tends it must have developed gradually from apelike
precursors.

One interesting piece of archaeological evidence also
seems to favor an early origin model for speech. It
comes from a study of some of the oldest-known stone
tools, carried out by Nicholas Toth of the University of
Indiana. Toth has established from patterns of flaking
that the earliest stone-toolmakers were mostly right-
handed, in roughly the same proportion as in modern
populations. Preferential handedness is unique to humans and is associated with laterality, the tendency of
the brain's two halves to concentrate on different aspects of cognition. In modern humans, control of language and fine motor movements is more heavily
focused in the left lobe—an indication, perhaps, that
handedness and language evolved at roughly the same
time.

More circumstantial reasons exist, too, for suspect-
ing that toolmaking and speech developed together.
Both are concerned with manipulating aspects of the
environment, the former physically, the latter symbolically. With both tools and language we take the world
apart, see its inner grain and come to regard it as a
collection of objects in space and time. For our convenience, and for the purposes of our survival, we
make the continuous discontinuous.

Language developed as a mutually-agreed-upon labeling system in which common features of the world
outside were identified by specific sounds. These were

mapped onto the brain and then mentally associated with appropriate images and other sensory impressions. At first, the most important words or intonations would probably have been those signaling various kinds of danger—as they are in many animal languages. "Look out!" is still one of the most immediately useful calls we can utter.

As soon as the rudiments of true spoken language began, selection would have come into play. Those individuals whose genes fortuitously supplied them with brains better able to recognize and produce vocalized sounds would have had a survival edge. Better brains meant bigger, more densely connected integration and association areas, notably in the prefrontal part of the brain. Growth of the prefrontal cortex added to the richness of man's internal reconstruction of nature and to his perception of the interrelationship between different facets of his surroundings. This, in turn, would have spurred on the development of his linguistic abilities, his talent for further categorization and his faculty for analyzing and controlling his environment.

Through language man was able to manipulate mentally what he saw, because language transformed the world "out there" into a rich inner domain of symbolic equivalents. A physical object, such as a log, might be hard or impossible for one person to move. But the labeled concept "log" could be played with at will—and at leisure. It could be set up in new positions, envisaged as a roller or a bridge or a boat. The symbol, the mental icon, had a freedom that the object itself lacked. Furthermore, once acquired, each new word joined the rest of man's burgeoning vocabulary so that it could be seen in juxtaposition with other symbol-equivalents abstracted from the real world.

At some point, this labeling process reached its climax. As humans increasingly learned to simulate the world in symbols, there must have come a time when the individual constructed a meaningful symbol for himself. Perhaps the switch from "wide-screen" experiential consciousness to an awareness centered on self took place swiftly, and even quite recently. One possibility is that the brain suddenly (in biological terms) flipped into a new, stable mode that gravitated around its internal symbolic representation of itself. Another scenario is that awareness of self grew only incrementally, over hundreds of thousands or even millions of years. Whichever is true, we can be sure that the feeling of being a particular individual brought with it considerable survival benefits, otherwise it would never have come about.

We are all descendants of those first "selfish" organisms that dwelt in earth's ancient ocean and, more latterly, of the hunting-gathering hominids in whose minds the shadows of self-awareness surely began to stir. Seen in this context, the emergence of identity has been an unbroken process of breathtaking scope and complexity. The thread of continuity from your present existence stretches back through ancestral generations to the dawn of humanity—and further, to the birth of the earth, the sun and the universe itself.

Yet on a more parochial level, your development began in the ovaries and testes of your parents. Here, during their own embryonic and fetal lives in the wombs of your grandmothers, those cells destined to form eggs and spermatozoa were first set aside as a special germ line. Subsequently these cells specialized, becoming the clearly identifiable forerunners of eggs and sperm. Early in the fetal life of your mother, the chromosomes within her egg precursor cells started an intricate process of genetic rearrangement. This culminated eventually in the production of eggs, each of which had only half the usual complement of chromosomes, each half-set being unique in the pattern and combination of genes it contained. The same kind of process took place in the development of your father's chromosomal contributions, albeit after his birth rather than before.

At the moment of your conception, your unique genetic program was brought together, in effect, by the toss of nature's dice, and then set running. Guided by your genes, still in the amniotic haze of preconsciousness, you developed in just forty weeks from a single, information-rich cell to a fetus containing a brain with about 100 billion neurons—effectively, the full adult human complement. Brain cells are not replaced like other cells of the body, nor are they added to much after birth. However, the sylphlike dendrites that form connections between brain cells—up to a thousand of them per neuron—do continue to change and reconfigure themselves throughout our lives. These slender branches and the nerve synapses (the microscopic gaps across which chemical signals influence neighboring cells) are crucial to the formation and functioning of the brain's internal maps—the maps that help us make sense of the world and of ourselves.

Much of the wiring of your brain took place while you were still in the womb. A typical fetal brain cell sprouts a main trunk, or axon, which then begins to grow and grope its way toward a specific target location in some other part of the brain. It does this by a kind of molecular sniffing. Each young axon has a specialized tip, called a growth cone, that can recognize a chemical trail laid down by other cells along the way. The target itself may also release chemical signals to tell the axon when it has arrived. But this is not the end of the story. Having reached the correct target, an axon still needs to find a particular "address," otherwise its connection will be faulty. However, unlike the pathway and target selection, address selection is much more hit-and-miss. In fact, axons have to fine-tune their connections by trial and error after birth, based on exposure to signals from the outside world.

Even while you were in the womb, your genes had only a general say in how your brain became wired. The huge number of brain cells and the vastly greater number of ways in which they could join together means that precise genetic control over every axon movement and dendritic branching is impossible. Gerald Edelman, Nobel laureate and head of the Rockefeller Neurosciences Institute in New York, has drawn an analogy between the brain and a rain forest, its vast flora of microscopic fronds, vines and arbors unrepeatably complex and unique.

Because you and I have thousands of tiny differences between our genes, the circuit diagrams of our brains are bound to be different. But they are very much more distinct because of the unpredictable ways in which individual neurons and groups of neurons subsequently develop, before and after birth.

During your early development, the massive number of circuits and potential signals in your synapses represented a kind of catalog of all potential human skills. This catalog has been built up and made available to all of us (with variations) through the evolution of our species. And it is from this great wealth of possibilities that your own specific environment and experience made their choice. A common fallacy is to assume that brain connections start to be laid down in earnest after birth. In fact, the opposite seems to be true. There are many more connections between nerve cells in an infant than in an adult. Development is more a matter of pruning than of proliferation.

After birth, connections between your neurons that were frequently stimulated survived and grew stronger; others atrophied or were switched to other tasks. Exposed to the particular circumstances of your childhood, specific orchestrations of cells were favored out of the colossal repertoire of possibilities. Gerald Edelman sees a parallel between this process and Darwinian selection in the world at large. According to this idea, the brain looks less like a rigidly programmed computer than an ecological habitat that mimics the evolution of life itself.

Some recent research in child development backs up this controversial new idea of dynamically evolving neuronal groups. Esther Thelsen, at the University of Indiana, has investigated how babies learn to reach. She found a wide variation among infants in the way they move their arms and legs to grab hold of an object. Over several months these patterns appeared to be in competition. Finally a number of successful strategies emerged. These strategies were always unique and adapted to the individual circumstances of each child.

The same winnowing process happens with language. During its first year or so of life, a baby babbles its way through almost every sound of every language. Later on, though, it loses the ability to make sounds that are not in its native tongue. An enormous range of sound patterns is available to us at birth, just as there is a huge variety of other potential skills waiting to be developed among the myriad unpruned circuits of the pristine brain. In the end, we learn to use only a few of them. But it is fascinating to speculate what else we might be capable of, given the appropriate nurturing.

The picture emerging is that individual brains and behavior patterns are governed far less by our genes than had previously been suspected. It may be that, in different people, the fetal neural maps carry a predisposition for aptitudes such as playing a musical instrument or math or strong hand-to-eye coordination. But if our brains subsequently evolve in Darwinian style, the development of such traits will depend to a large degree on the actual life experiences of a child. Each of us, then, is very much an individual, molded more by nurture than by nature—a unique creation in a highly creative world.

THE "I" OF ILLUSION

"Unless you know what it is, I ain't never going to
be able to explain it to you."

—*Louis Armstrong, on jazz*

*W*e have an overwhelming sense of self, of being a
particular, permanent focus of being. Our experience
is powerfully "I"-centered. We assume we know im-
plicitly what this "I" is and, therefore, that questions
such as Will I survive death? are meaningful and must
have a definite (if as yet unknown) answer.

We think of the "I" within us as being central and
transcendent, as Descartes did, because this is just the
way it feels. A single, inner voice seems to shape our
thoughts, to make choices and pass judgments. It con-
vinces us that we exist as individuals. It is us, our

personalized selves, the free-floating observer in the brain. And yet it may also be a most extraordinary illusion.

"I think, therefore I am," declared Descartes. However, recent dramatic experimental results, such as those achieved by Benjamin Libet, a physiologist at the University of California at Los Angeles, challenge the notion that there is a Cartesian observer, a localized "I" inside our heads, watching and controlling everything we do.

Over the past decade or so, Libet has been steadily amassing evidence that suggests it may take up to half a second for our conscious impressions of the world to form. The feeling we have of living in the present, in fact, may be just a clever trick, and we can only really know about events, even those over which we were sure we had exercised conscious control, after they have already happened.

One of Libet's experiments involved connecting subjects to an EEG and asking them to flex their wrist spontaneously at any moment they felt the urge. He found that the subjects showed a readiness potential—a sharp drop in electrical activity in the brain that serves to clear the way for a neural event—a full half-second before any wrist flexions occurred. Even more surprising, this readiness potential showed up a good three hundred milliseconds before subjects reported consciously experiencing any impulse to make a move.

In a second test, a light touch on the hand of the subject was followed by a second stimulus, an electrical impulse, direct to the part of the brain that maps sensations for touch. Libet found that if the direct impulse followed four hundred milliseconds after the touch, the two stimuli merged and were experienced as a single, heightened response. Crucially, not only was the lapse in time between the two events not noticed, but the combined event felt as if it had happened a half-second earlier. From the subject's point of view, the experience was timed to the moment the hand was touched rather than to when the brain was directly stimulated.

Libet sums up these astonishing results like this: "The brain seems to be able to compensate for the lag in its processing. It can refer everything that happened backward in time to the moment it [the stimulus] first arrived at the brain so that, subjectively, it feels as if we are living in the immediate present."

Evidently, brain events take an unexpectedly long time to bubble up and form a coherent picture. Much of our thinking, reacting and decision-making takes place at a subconscious level, with consciousness only seeming to do all the work and only seeming to act in concert with stimuli and responses.

Libet's work ties in well with the experience of athletes whose sports demand accurate split-second decisions. Tennis players frequently talk of being "zoned," when their minds attain a Zenlike wordlessness and their shots flow with fluid grace. What they appear to be doing in this state is blocking the distracting chatter of conscious thought, putting consciousness in the backseat and allowing their brains to be given over fully to subconscious processing.

Support for this idea comes from an experiment by University of California at Berkeley psychologist Arthur Jensen. He asked a group of volunteers to deliberately delay their responses in a reaction-time test by as short an interval as possible. Their reaction times were found to increase not marginally but by a big jump—from 250 milliseconds to 600 or 700 milliseconds. Apparently, the need to wait for consciousness to make a decision is what causes this disjointed delay, a result which suggests that allowing consciousness to take control of a skilled action such as a tennis return will lead to a clumsy, jerky response. Science, it seems, has found the answer to another of those great sporting mysteries—why even a grand-slam pro is apt to swat a tempting lob wildly out of court or drill it into the bottom of the net. With the ball hanging in the air for so long, consciousness has time to catch up with events and then, like an overzealous novice, rushes in and makes a complete hash of what otherwise would have been the easiest of winners.

On a more profound level, Libet's results expose the fatal flaw in Descartes's *"Cogito . . ."*—that is, the belief that there is a pontifical "I" holding court at some specific site within the brain. Neurologist Daniel Dennett, head of the Center for Cognitive Studies at Tufts University, has attacked this notion as "the most tenacious bad idea bedeviling our attempts to think about consciousness." Research such as Libet's shows there is no precise instant when the brain becomes aware of a stimulus. This failure, Dennett claims, demolishes the long-held concept of the Cartesian "I" inhabiting the brain.

How can there be a privileged ghost or homunculus watching from inside the brain-machine if it cannot time when it "knows" about an event so that it can decide to tell the brain what to do or say in response? New research on speech production also casts doubt on the theory that posits a central "meaner" who decides what "I" think and then orders the mouth to utter the desired words. The novelist E. M. Forster was there first when he sniped, "How do I know what I think till I see what I say?"

Dennett advocates connectionism as a key to further progress. Connectionism argues that the brain is an enormously complex parallel processing machine. At any moment, many neural networks are simultaneously at work handling incoming information. Different networks take precedence at different times as alarm bells ring. Effectively, it is as if hordes of homunculi were clamoring and competing for attention, each specializing in a different aspect of perception. As they go about their tasks, they confer with one another and form coalitions, producing drafts of the raw data they take in. The process goes on ceaselessly: information entering the nervous system is under continuous editorial revision, so that at any point in time there are multiple drafts of narrative fragments at various stages of editing scattered about the brain. Ultimately, Dennett says,

"we" experience this as a single narrative—a coherent, unified stream of consciousness—in the same way
that our eyes seem to bring us a clear, steady image of
the world although they jiggle around like handheld
cameras.

Self may be a sleight of the brain. But that doesn't
make it any less important from a subjective viewpoint.
A chair reduces to a near-empty cloud of particles at
the subatomic level but is evidently still solid enough to
sit on. Who is to say when one thing is more real than
another? The "I" inside each of us exists in the sense
that we undeniably feel like individuals, distinct and
different from all others. Perhaps Descartes should be
paraphrased: "I think as if I am, therefore I am!"

When we ask whether there is life after death, we
usually mean "Does the ego, the 'real me,' continue in
some form?" In other words, can the experience of
self-consciousness persist after the brain stops working—after it literally "gives up the ghost"? This, points
out mathematician and philosopher Martin Gardner, is
the crux of the debate as far as most people are concerned. "Personal immortality," he has written, "has
nothing to do with living on through descendants and
friends, or living in future records of the past. It has
nothing to do with surviving through achievements
in science, literature, music, or art. . . . A person does
not acquire immortality by identifying himself or herself with the human race, even if one makes the dubious assumption that the race will never become

extinct.'' Immortality, Gardner insists, requires on-going consciousness of personal identity and personal memories.

One of the hallmarks of consciousness is that it seems so strongly localized in the individual. "I" go to sleep in my forty-year-old body in the north of England, surrounded by familiar people and things, and wake up feeling, as always, like "me," in more or less the same state. I never find myself in the brain of an Amazonian tribesman or an Icelandic barmaid, seeing the world from a totally different perspective. I never look out through unfamiliar eyes, or (consciously at least) share another's thoughts. I seem to be firmly stuck inside this particular body and brain.

But what of identical twins? From an early age, we grasp the meaning of identity and diversity in the world outside and in our own persons. We come to recognize our uniqueness as individuals. Yet in the case of identical twins, identity and diversity coincide. Could it be that such persons, in a sense, experience a single overlapping consciousness rather than two entirely separate selves?

Identical twins display a fascinating mirror symmetry. If one twin has a birthmark on the right cheek, the other often bears it on the left; if one's right eye is slightly darker than the left, the opposite is true for his co-twin; right-handedness in one implies left-handedness in the other. Yet the parallels seem to extend far beyond mere physical equivalence, with occasionally remarkable results.

On March 11, 1979, the *Chicago Tribune* reported on the reunion of twins who, having been adopted at birth, had been brought up separately and had lived apart for thirty-nine years. In spite of not having seen each other in all that time, each had married a woman named Linda and then divorced; each named a son James Allan; each then married a woman named Betty. Their hobbies—mechanical lettering and carpentry— were the same; their favorite resort was the same beach in the St. Petersburg area of Florida; their occupations were similar.

When we look at other people, we see beings who are obviously like us in some ways and who on many occasions, reason insists, must have similar thoughts. An identical twin, however, sees not just similarity but sameness—as if he were "beside himself," his consciousness shared.

Mark Twain summed up the twins' dilemma with customary insight and wit. Speaking to a journalist, he remarked that he had been born one member of a twin pair. Tragedy had struck soon after, however, when one of the twins, left unattended in the bathtub, drowned. As the two brothers were almost indistinguishable, even the parents had trouble telling who had died and who had survived. Years later, Twain delved into the circumstances of the event and came to examine the hospital records. In these he found that the attending physician had noted a birthmark on his brother's back. Now, since he, Mark Twain, knew of the existence of a birthmark on his own back, he was driven to a mind-bending conclusion. "It is he who survived," Twain declared. "I drowned."

A thought experiment brings the philosophical paradox of twins into still sharper relief. Imagine—it may someday even be technically possible—that a person is created who is identical to you in every way. This creature not only looks like you, but every particle in his body, down to the last atom, is in the same relative position and state. Every memory, every thought of your synthetic twin is the same at the instant of creation as your own. The moment the twin appears, what would it be like for you? Would you continue to be aware only of your old self looking out on the world from your old vantage point? Or would you now have a kind of dual consciousness, an awareness emanating from two different physical locations?

An initial reaction might be to suppose that you would be unaffected by the appearance of the twin. You would simply see an exact copy of yourself, be somewhat amazed at the experience, but then shrug your shoulders and carry on with life as if nothing untoward had happened. Your copy, meanwhile, would have his own distinct consciousness that, although it might feel exactly like yours, would be experienced by him alone.

This account fails, however, to do justice to the problem. The fact is, the replica of yourself would be as much "you" as you! To maintain absolute identity, we could arrange for the twin to materialize instantly facing you in the center of an empty, symmetrical room. His first sensory experience would then be the same as yours down to the last detail. There would be *no difference whatsoever* between you and him. Nor could you claim to be somehow privileged on the grounds that you were there first; the inescapable truth is, you would be on an equal footing from the moment the twin appeared. Given these conditions, if you insist that you would still be the ''old you'' and that your exactly identical twin would have a separate consciousness of his own (which you would not be privy to), then the onus is on you to explain how this could be so. Logically, because there would be no difference between you and your duplicate, there ought to be no difference in the experience of self; you would be he and he would be you. The implication is that your consciousness would be replicated along with your brain and body. You would effectively reside in two people at once.

Quite how this would feel is hard to say since it would be an experience unique in human history. But perhaps the often-reported shared mental bonds of real twins offer some clues. Identical twins frequently seem to know, intuitively, what is happening to the other, especially if one of the pair is in mortal danger. There are even stories of physical pain felt by one twin being somehow registered simultaneously by the other over great distances. Nor is this experience of shared consciousness necessarily confined to twins. Reports of people accurately sensing the death of close family members or friends, over thousands of miles, are not uncommon. Anecdotal though these accounts may be, they are evidently given in good faith and occur often enough to be taken seriously.

Returning to our thought experiment, what would happen next if the two exactly identical yous were to leave the room by different doors and enter an outside world that was highly asymmetrical? Say that one of the twins is driven off in a taxi and then flown to the Bahamas, while the other goes to an office job in the city. Thereafter they live entirely dissimilar lives. From the moment of departure from the symmetrical room, the experiences of the twins would begin to diverge so that their mental states and recently formed memories would also start to move apart. What would it feel like now to be you? Several possibilities present themselves, each with its problems.

The first is that you end up being both the twins. Your consciousness, in other words, is the sum consciousness of both individuals. This follows on from our earlier logic, but seems to run into increasing difficulties the longer the twins are apart. Different experiences will mold the twins in different ways, so that they become more and more distinguishable in their appearance and behavior. How can the twins be different people and the same person at the same time?

The second possibility is that you are just one of the twins, that is, what was you becomes once again localized within a single body. The trouble here is that your relationship to each of the twins leaving the room is exactly similar. Because of this there are no grounds for saying that you are one rather than the other.

The third option is that you are neither of the resultant people. But this is perhaps the least acceptable of all because it implies that by creating a copy of yourself you destroy the original!

On balance, we are led to admit that the first possibility—that two yous are created—is the most likely. However, by entertaining that it may be possible to replicate self-consciousness, we have begun to subtly alter our concept of the nature of self and of awareness as a whole.

Take another case. Imagine that in some far-future time, long after your death, an exact copy of you in your present state, reading this book, is manufactured. Would that "new you" really be you? Would it feel as if you had simply woken up after having "fallen asleep" at the point of death? Evidently not, since this new you would have only your present memories and neural connections and none of those which you will accumulate (or lose) between now and your death. Continuity of consciousness, then, would be ruled out. Would, instead, the new you feel exactly as you do now? This does not seem quite right either. The old you lived out his life and died. How can a new version of you be fashioned, through which you can live again with your consciousness "rewound" to some arbitrary point?

These strange thought experiments are not entirely without practical bearing. For those who have opted to be deep-frozen after death, the question of who is going to be inside their heads if and when they are ever revived is presumably of some concern. Leaving aside the monstrous technical problems of repairing or replacing tens of billions of badly damaged brain cells, there is the more delicate issue of what happens if the person who becomes conscious when the frozen brain is restored is not the same as the one who handed over his life-insurance policy to the cryonics company. Could the cryonaut's descendants sue? And if this re-animated person proves not to be the one that died, then exactly who is he? What would it be like for him or her suddenly to be made conscious, without a real past and, apparently, an identity to relate to?

Our appearance, abilities, memories, values and opinions all contribute to making us the unique individuals we are. But there are other crucial aspects to being a "self": a stored impression of continuity and an awareness of existing at a single, forward-moving moment of time—the ever-present now.

"We" are constantly changing. We grow, age, add and lose memories, alter our opinions, become wiser or more foolish. Even the very particles of which we are made are continually being replaced—all are probably different now than they were, say, ten years ago. But it is not these objective qualities that lie at the heart of the mystery. It is the subjective, experiential side of self that proves so perplexing.

At forty, I look and think differently than when I was four or fourteen. Yet not only am I understood by others to be the same person, but I feel inwardly to be the same. My memories extend back in time linking me with that succession of younger men and boys who, though distinct in many ways, were still somehow "myself."

I go to sleep and self-awareness (except to some extent in dreams) shuts off. But there it is again when I awake. Because "I" am not there when self-consciousness is absent, I fail to notice the passage of time. Eight hours elapse while I am in bed but they are as nothing.

We do not fear losing consciousness if we can be reasonably assured of continuing where we left off when consciousness is restored. In this respect, both sleep, in which we spend about a third of our lives, and general anesthesia are acceptable. But, if it could be arranged, how would we feel about becoming our past or future selves? Then the prospect would seem more daunting. In such a situation, we would not be able to preserve our present cargo of memories or, more important, our present sense of self. It might be like becoming a stranger—and that is frightening, because to become someone else is to lose yourself.

That is precisely why we are afraid of dying. Death threatens to dissolve our selves permanently, a possibility we simply cannot come to grips with. What would it be like to be nothing? The Greek philosopher Lucretius pointed the way to an answer as early as the first century B.C. The eternity after death, he said, is simply the mirror image of the eternity before birth.

No one finds it disturbing to contemplate the prenatal state, so why should they be alarmed about the eternity to come? Fifteen billion years had already gone by before you appeared on the scene. But the wait was not terrifying because, to the "un-you," there was no wait. Likewise, if you permanently cease to exist in a few decades' time, you will not be around to worry about the billions of years to come. As far as you are concerned, the remaining span of the universe will be over in an instant. Seneca summed it up: "What is death? Either a transition or an end. I am not afraid of coming to an end, this being the same as never having begun, nor of transition, for I shall never be in confinement quite as cramped anywhere else as I am here."

And what about the process of dying itself, the actual transition from life to death? Is that something to fear? As the German philosopher Ludwig Wittgenstein reasoned: "Death is not an event in life; we do not experience death."

So, in fact, there is no rational basis at all for our fear of death. We shall either remain conscious in some form or feel nothing at all. And what is there to be afraid of in that? Yet, like someone who refuses to be consoled in the dentist's waiting room, most of us are afraid, enormously. We are terrified of the unknown and what it might be like not to have a self.

We build up the self inside us to be something tremendously important, a solid, secure hub around which our lives can revolve. And yet how easily this feeling of self can be made to melt away. Turn on some of your favorite music or, better still, play it. Watch a good film, ride a switchback, make love, meditate. Where is your sense of self in the midst of any of these distractions? Self dissolves a thousand times a day, only to be quickly reconstituted from stored memories and a kind of neural bootstrap process; thus the brain works hard to keep the narrative or stream of consciousness flowing smoothly, convincing us of the continuity of our selves.

What happens, though, when that continuity is blown apart, by injury, disease or psychological disorder? Then our familiar world can seem to collapse or fragment.

Documentary accounts such as *The Three Faces of Eve, Sybil* and *The Minds of Billy Milligan* brought the extraordinary condition known as multiple personality into full public view. Through great psychological and physical trauma, such as extreme abuse as a child, it seems that a person's self can be made to break apart so that, effectively, more than one individual share the same brain. In the past, many psychiatrists dismissed "multiples" as clever fakes or misdiagnosed their condition as schizophrenia. But it seems clear now that the disorder, though quite rare, is indisputably real.

The first strong evidence that the various personalities of a sufferer are associated with genuinely distinct patterns of brain activity came in 1982. Frank Putnam, a psychiatrist working for the National Institute of Mental Health at Bethesda, Maryland, measured the "evoked potential," the brain response to a specific visual stimulus, for each of four personalities of ten patients. He found that while all the brain-wave patterns of the personalities, for a given patient, fell within the normal range, they were as different from one another as the patterns of two different human subjects.

We often wonder what it would be like to be someone else, to "get inside" another person's head. Those who are unfortunate enough to harbor multiple personalities know—though from their point of view the experience is far from desirable.

On one occasion, for instance, "Sybil" was waiting for an elevator in a hall at Columbia University, in New York City, only to find herself, apparently the next moment, outside, late at night in a strange, inhospitable neighborhood of a city she at first did not recognize. Five days had elapsed without her knowledge and she was in Philadelphia with a hotel key in her pocket that she had never seen before. She had flipped from her depleted core self into one of her fifteen alternative personalities and back again and knew nothing of the time for which "she" had been gone.

This, then, is what it would be like to be a completely different person—nothing at all. If you were another person, then "you" would not be there to share or remember the experience. Upon becoming yourself again, it would be as if no time had passed. You can never know from another person's subjective viewpoint what it feels like to be him.

Victims of multiple personality disorder can receive

psychiatric treatment to help overcome their condition. In time, the various sundered fragments of the individual can be brought back into common awareness again and merged. Thus the person's self can once more be made whole. Physical damage to the brain, however, is often irreparable.

In *The Man with a Shattered World,* the psychiatrist A. R. Luria told the remarkable and deeply disturbing story of Lyova Zasetsky, a student who was called up following the German invasion of the Soviet Union. During the battle of Smolensk, in early 1943, Zasetsky was hit in the head by a machine-gun bullet. The injury and later complications destroyed large parts of his brain. At first he could remember nothing, not even his name, nor could he read or write or recognize anyone. "I seemed," he commented later, "to be some sort of newborn creature that just looked, listened, observed, repeated, but still had no mind of its own."

Luria wrote: "He no longer had any sense of space, could not judge relationships between things, and perceived the world as broken into thousands of separate parts." It was as if Zasetsky the inner man had ceased to exist. As he wrote chillingly in his journal: "I was killed March 2, 1943."

Stroke, or more insidious conditions such as Alzheimer's disease, can also permanently rob the brain of crucial functions, cutting us adrift from our future and our past. In some cases, when highly specific parts of the brain are affected, the results can be bizarre.

A rare condition called face agnosia impairs only a

victim's ability to recognize faces, leaving all other mental functions intact. Neurologist Antonio Damasio, at the University of Iowa College of Medicine, has spent the past twenty years investigating such cases. He recalls, for instance, the plight of a female patient who, having suffered a stroke in the night, awoke unable to recognize the faces of her husband and daughter. Although she still knew who they were by their voices and mannerisms, their faces were like those of complete strangers to her. Damasio tested her powers of reasoning, memory, reading ability and vision, and found them all to be normal. Yet she could no longer either identify or learn to identify the faces of relatives and friends she had known for years.

Using advanced scanning techniques, Damasio and his wife, Hanna, a neurologist and anatomist, have pinpointed the affected areas of the brain. These are what Damasio has christened "convergence zones"— regions in which circuits of neurons processing visual information merge with other streams of sensory data, such as the sound of someone's voice, the perceived tone of his skin or the appearance of his gestures. The convergence zones, in turn, are wired to higher centers in the brain handling memory function and storage.

The various levels of connections normally act in concert to produce that overall sense of familiarity we feel when we look at someone we know. But in victims of face agnosia, the recognition circuit is severed at some key junction. These people still retain the general concept of faces and the ability to understand and re-

spond appropriately to such expressions as anger, sad-
ness and joy. "The breakdown," Damasio says, "is at
the level of uniqueness."

To test his conclusions, Damasio used an instrument
akin to a lie detector to measure the skin conductance
responses of four patients suffering from acute face
agnosia. He showed his subjects a series of photos of
people they knew well. In every case, the patients
reacted in a way which showed that some form of
recognition was taking place at a subconscious level,
even though they couldn't say out loud to whom the
faces belonged.

Damasio believes such subconscious activity may be
the trigger that, in most of us, starts off a chain reaction
of orchestrated responses that ultimately results in us
identifying a particular face. "Recognition in the true
sense must be conscious," he asserts.

In a more extreme condition, known as "blind
sight," victims report having no sense of vision at all.
However, tests reveal that not only are their eyes working perfectly well, but the fine bundles of neurons
joining the retinas to the appropriate regions in the
visual cortex are also correctly in place. Again, the
break in the system seems to be at a higher, integrative
level where the various aspects of a visual field come
together before being presented, neatly packaged, to
our awareness. Eerily, blind-sight patients can see but
don't know it.

The more we learn about the brain, the more it
seems "we" are cast in the role of passengers rather

than pilots. So much goes on automatically without "our" involvement. The latest scan techniques reveal the brain to be like a society of specialists whose existence we would never normally suspect. One particular grape-sized region deals only with regular verbs, another with irregular verbs. The degree of specialization is that great. Yet, after many stages of cross-connection and convergence, all these diverse aspects of processing and perception are brought together as a unified consciousness. And there, at the top of the hierarchy, doing the watching, is our self. We have this impression from the inside, of being an entity that sits apart from the brainworks like a spectator at a ball game. But, in fact, "we" are smeared all over the brain. The self as a fixed, central observer is an illusion, a phantasm that through malfunction of its supporting structure can be diminished or destroyed.

An important part of our experience of self is our ability to project backward in time, to lay down and access memories at will. But what happens when that recall ability is lost?

Clive Wearing once enjoyed an international reputation as a specialist in Renaissance music. But in 1985 he was struck down by a rare brain infection caused by herpes simplex, the same virus responsible for cold sores. As a result, large numbers of neurons, especially in his hippocampal lobes, were wiped out. Lying deep within the brain, the hippocampus works to consolidate recently acquired information, turning short-term memory into long-term. Deprived of this vital midway

station between the cortex and the more primal regions of the brain, Clive Wearing lost his sense of past
time. As his wife explains: "Clive's world now consists
of a moment, with no past to anchor it to and no future
to look forward to." Every minute of every day he is
under the illusion of having just woken from a deep
sleep—a situation his diary graphically reveals:

  9:04 A.M. Now I am AWAKE
  10:00 A.M. NOW I AM AWAKE
  10:28 A.M. ACTUALLY I AM NOW FIRST
    TIME AWAKE for years
  10:54 A.M. Now I am awake for the first time

Clive Wearing suffers from Korsakoff's syndrome, a
condition first documented by the Russian physician of
that name in 1887. In this nightmarish state, victims
lose the ability to lay down new memories and, as a
result, are effectively trapped in time. The consequences can be bizarre, as Oliver Sacks describes in his
book *The Man Who Mistook His Wife for a Hat*. For
example, there was the case of "Mr. Thompson":
"He remembered nothing for more than a few seconds. He was completely disoriented. Abysses of am-
nesia continually opened up beneath him, but he would
bridge them, mainly by fluent confabulations and fictions of all kinds. For him they were not fictions, but
how he suddenly saw or interpreted the world . . .
[He] must literally make himself and his world up every
moment."

Cases such as these speak of more than just the fragile and constructed nature of self. They raise serious questions about the nature of time and of the delicate connection between psychological time and physical reality. Could it be that time, like self, is nothing more than a product of the way we think?

ANYONE FOR *T*?

"In any attempt to bridge the domains of experience belonging to the spiritual and philosophical sides of our nature, time occupies a key position."

—*Sir Arthur Stanley Eddington*

*T*he naive Christian concept of heaven seems idyllic on the face of it. After death, your private soul with its self-identity intact is free to wander peacefully around beautiful gardens and leafy glades meeting happy, smiling people. No crime, no risk of accident, everything laid on. And just imagine what great characters of the past (and the future) you might run into—Einstein, Lincoln, Shakespeare, Bach—albeit that the vast majority of the heavenly host would be less auspicious folk like you and me. As George Bernard Shaw once re-marked, "In heaven an angel is no one in particular."

Yes, it would be nice to be in paradise—for a while. The problem is, it wouldn't end. Days there would stretch into weeks, weeks into years, and years into centuries. The novelty, it seems, would be bound to wear off. Yet still you would be obliged to stay in this cosy, tranquil place populated by kindly souls like yourself. And the centuries would become millennia, and the millennia would become trillions upon trillions of years, because this is the life everlasting—the endless treadmill of the hereafter. In our desperation for a dash of excitement, a bit of daredevilry, we might almost be tempted to side with Mark Twain: "Heaven for climate, hell for company." The problem is—time; there's just too much of it in eternity.

On earth, by comparison, time always seems to be in short supply. We ride atop the wave crest of now between the unreachable and knowable past and the reachable and unknowable future, prisoners of the present. But the present is always moving, carrying us helplessly forward to meet our destiny—and, ultimately, our death.

We live in a time-obsessed society. Get up, get dressed, wolf down breakfast, dash to work, do the job, try to beat the rush hour home, and finally collapse for an all-too-brief while before going to bed, ready to start the whole cycle again. For most of us, the day, the week, the year, our whole lives are mapped out for us by the need to stay in step with the rest of the world. The watch on our wrist, the clock on the wall, the bleeping alarm or pager warn us that the next appointment is already fast approaching. And all the while, the seconds of our life's story tick remorselessly away. Two hundred and thirty-five million of them, or thereabouts, at birth, reducing by 86,400 with each day that passes. And, worryingly, time gathers pace, or appears to, the more our lives progress.

In childhood, a hot summer's day can seem endless, whereas by middle age our birthdays race around again with alarming speed. We notice the same effect on a long vacation; the first few days seem unusually long, while later days fly by.

It may be, in part, that our brain derives its subjective measure of time by how often novel additions are made to its memory. When we are young and everything is new, the days seem stretched out because they are filled with so many new, "memorable" events. But as we grow older, routine sets in and the brain, with fewer fresh experiences to file away, compresses time and so speeds the apparent passage of our lives.

Then, too, there is evidence that the biological clock within each of us—the hormonal regulating mechanism responsible for circadian rhythms—slows down as we age. Less frequent "ticks" from our body's metronome would create the illusion of time passing more quickly.

Other factors can affect the rate at which time seems to flow. LSD accelerates perceived time (as well as causing gross spatial distortions); tranquilizers retard it. Time seems to flow with peculiar variability in dreams and, similarly, under clinical hypnosis subjects can be influenced to perceive time as passing either more slowly or more quickly. During the commonly reported ''life review'' of near-death experiences, time can appear telescoped down to almost nothing, while other extreme temporal dislocations are associated with certain mental disorders and diseases of the brain.

Radical changes in the perception of time are often described by psychotic patients. Schizophrenics, for instance, may grossly underestimate their age or the period of their confinement. Effectively, they suffer a loss of time-consciousness.

Brain damage, inflicted by accident or disease, can have an equally devastating effect. Acute loss of short-term memory and other brain functions can totally sever an individual's links to the past and the future. For them, it is as if time has ceased to flow.

All this suggests that, at the very least, there is a strong psychological component to our experience of moving through time. Our ability to make and access memories and to speculate about the future plays a crucial role in our perception of time flow. Once these links are broken, each moment appears in isolation, like a single frame from a world in which time as we know it no longer exists.

Time and mind, it seems, are inextricably linked. Could it be that, in the absence of all record-keeping, self-conscious observers such as ourselves, the universe would be completely timeless? In other words, is moving time a pure fabrication of our brain's ability to make sense of disparate events or does it have a true and independent basis in reality?

Origins again. The evolution of human language and the development of our sense of self, we saw earlier, probably occurred hand in hand, the one feeding off the other. Language allowed man to internalize and rationalize the world in a remarkable new way—as a complex montage of discrete, labeled objects and events. But the flood of facts and discordant images that this fresh outlook on nature made available must surely have threatened the brain with overload and chaos. Some powerful organizing agency was needed to enable our ancestors to make sense of the piecemeal universe now gradually being revealed to them. And, in response, time may have entered human awareness.

Smoothly flowing, unidirectional time is the means by which man's brain orders its memories. As language rose to preeminence, time became the sequencing device by which subjective, verbally encoded events and experiences could be sorted and stored coherently. Time gave us a map by which to find our way around in the confusion of reductionist space.

But, coincidentally, time emphasized the individual. It did this because consciousness of self depends upon having a clear sense of personal continuity through a succession of different states of awareness. Language and the subjective perception of flowing time and self-consciousness are mutually interdependent, so that inevitably they must have come about together.

Not all human cultures, however, have perceived time in quite the same way. The ebb and flow of tides, the recurrence of the seasons and the wheeling movements of sun, moon and stars give the powerful impression that nature turns endlessly full circle. Because of this, early man and early civilizations almost certainly regarded time as being cyclical. We know that the Maya of Central America, for instance, believed that history would repeat itself every 260 years, the so-called *lamat,* a fact that the Spanish conquistadors were not slow to exploit in the timing of their invasion. In Hindu cosmology, the entire universe is thought to cycle between birth, death and rebirth every 4,320,000,000 years, or one *kalpa,* an impressive enough time span even by contemporary astronomical standards (and close, incidentally, to the age of the earth).

Greek philosophers and cosmologists, too, embraced the notion of perpetual repetition. As Aristotle wrote in his great work *Physics,* "There is a circle in all things that have natural movement and coming into being and passing away . . . Even time is thought to be a circle."

Jewish and Christian teachings, however, shattered the concept of this ancient cycle of time. The myth of the fall from Eden speaks of a unique, never-to-be-repeated beginning of time and history, the moment when man, having eaten of the forbidden Tree of Knowledge, learns the bitter truth about his own mortality. Thus, wrapped in this parable for the masses is the chronicle of the passing from circular to linear time.

Christianity, with its emphasis on the birth and death of Christ and the crucifixion as once-only events, further underscored the notion of time as a straight path that stretched from the past to the future. So the mind of Western man became primed for the idea of progress and evolution—an idea that, paradoxically, led to the eventual schism between religion, with its timeless spiritual teachings, and science, with its progressive search for physical truth.

For the average person in the Middle Ages of Europe, progress of any sort must have been hard to discern. In the midst of such a firmly entrenched caste system, a static hierarchy from lowliest serf to monarch, the life of the peasant was unrelentingly the same, year in, year out. The psyche of the common man, tied as it was to the land and the seasonal rhythms, would still have retained much of the ancient feel for nature's endless, organic cycles.

But all that was about to change. With the dawn of the Renaissance and the coming of the Age of Exploration in the sixteenth and seventeenth centuries, a great search began for new markets and raw materials. Shortly afterward, in mid-eighteenth-century England, the harnessing of steam empowered the Industrial Revolution, so that within little more than a generation the lives of countless ordinary folk in the developing West were altered beyond recognition. The focus of society shifted abruptly from agriculture to industry and commerce. The entrenched sense of repetition in time, based on the annual reappearance of plants, swiftly faded from mainstream awareness to be replaced by an insatiable desire for growth and change. Whereas agricultural institutions can afford to be static, those centered on commerce feed on growth as a means of generating new wealth. Capitalism had arrived and with it the yearning for material acquisition and progress. In the wake of the Industrial Revolution, the idea of change for one's self and family came to be seen as natural and necessary. No longer, in this new, industrialized society, were there rigid barriers to the upwardly mobile.

Protestantism, too, was on the march, with its underlying ethos of hard work and self-improvement. So, borne along by a tidal wave of secular developments, Western religion became ever more strongly wedded to the notion of linear time. Just as Catholicism embraced fewer formal and repetitive rituals than did Judaism, so Protestantism abandoned many of the rigid, cyclical traditions prescribed by Rome.

By the nineteenth century, the idea in the West of temporal succession came to assume even greater importance in daily human life and thought. The fruits of the Industrial Revolution were now everywhere to be seen, while, on a different front, Charles Darwin's theory of evolution through natural selection made linear time the backdrop for the development of life itself. It is no coincidence that the same era also saw the rapid evolution of the novel and the autobiography.

Nor has this rush toward the future since slowed. To-day, more than ever, we seem committed to a policy of accelerating material progress, change and develop-ment, with scant regard for our spiritual growth.

We live our daily lives in a realm of causality, with a past and a future, governed by the clock. Here, in this ubiquitous device, is the very embodiment of linearity and sequence. Inside the clock, the to-and-fro rotation of a wheel or the vibrations of a crystal are translated into smooth movements of a pointer. The more con-stant the internal mechanism, the better, for one sec-ond must be defined as the equal of any other in true linear time. According to the clock, one event follows another in strict, unvarying sequence; four o'clock al-ways follows three and precedes five. The consistent, one-moment-after-another sequence of clock time is so much a received part of normal awareness that we accept it as stemming directly from the way time "really is."

Certainly, our perceived sense of linear, sequential time is successful in terms of getting things done in our kind of society. It lets us plan for the future and co-ordinate our individual and social lives. It is the basis for precise timing of events in any scientific enquiry.

But the gathering acceptance in the West of a linear basis for time has also had a profoundly negative effect. It has strengthened still further our sense of separation and of ego-consciousness. Consequently, death has be-come something to fear because it marks a unique, never-to-be-repeated occurrence—the potential extinction of our selves. No longer do we find solace in the notion of regeneration and rebirth, now that the wheel of time has been stilled. Our divorce from the cosmic cycles has resulted in a loss of our sense of communion with nature. And the effect of this has been devastating to our collective psyche.

At this stage in our history, to a greater extent than ever before, we construct sharp boundaries between our selves and the rest of the world. From an early age we are encouraged to see ourselves as different from other people, with our own unique personality and skills. The more we are treated as an individual, the more we become like one because our sense of self is based largely on how others relate and react to us. As children we are free, innocent of our limitations in time and space. A child lives each moment as if it were the only one. But as we grow older, our ego boundaries increasingly wall us in from our surroundings. Coincidentally, we become aware that every day is not the same, that death exists and that we are moving inexorably toward it.

We have reached, it seems, a crisis point in our cultural development. Our reasoning, forward-looking brain tells us that death is inevitable. Yet whereas in previous ages the individual saw herself as just another part of nature's self-regenerative cycle, now we find ourselves with no such conceptual safety net. We have built up the importance of our selves, while at the same time we have become subjectively decoupled from the global cycles of life. We feel alone, in a vast, apparently uncaring universe, chained to egos that are terrified of dying. And worse, we have largely lost faith in the religions that once held out the promise of an afterlife. What is left? We can look to medical science for a way of extending life and postponing the fateful day. Or we can bury ourselves in the kind of pseudo-scientific nonsense that nowadays is peddled as a substitute for true religion.

But always, at the back of our mind, is the certainty of death and the looming threat of personal dissolution. We know now, too, that this seemingly robust self inside our heads can be altered or chipped away or destroyed completely by physical changes to the brain. Our sense of self, modern neurology tells us, is an artifact of the human cortex—nothing more. The self is not the soul; there *is* no personal, immortal soul, the new high priests of science insist. Descartes and the other dualists and the Christian theologians were wrong all along. When the brain dies, the self dies. And when the self dies, so do we. "We must accept," says Gerald Edelman, "that death means the irrevocable loss of an individual and that individual's being." Most contemporary neurologists would agree. In Daniel Dennett's words: "Materialism of one sort or another is now a received opinion, approaching unanimity."

Sadly, our response to this modern denial of the soul only makes matters worse. We bury the problem by staying busy, working harder, trying to acquire greater material wealth, "security" and positions of power. We compete with our fellows from an early age for possessions and status. But in so doing we only strengthen and extend the boundaries of our ego-selves. What we own and even who we know become, in a sense, part of our selves. Losing someone or something dear to us is then a painful wrench, not so much because we are sorry for whoever is gone (though that may also be true), but because we ourselves have been diminished—a small part of us has died. Paradoxically, because of this, the more powerful and extensive our egos become, the more vulnerable and insecure we feel.

We are not alone among living things in having extended selves. The spider has its web, the snail its shell, and there are countless other animals and plants whose effective selves extend well beyond their physical bodies. In the case of a social insect such as an ant, we may even go so far as to treat an entire colony of creatures, which individually are incapable of survival, as a single superorganism—a sort of corporate self embracing perhaps millions of separate biological units.

But with modern man the scale of the "selfish" phenomenon has reached outrageous proportions. A rich individual may own a number of lavish homes, cars and many other expensive pieces of property and have great monetary wealth, all of which becomes absorbed in the extended self and none of which is strictly necessary for survival. The rich, however, die on schedule along with the poor.

Possessions have become another of our ploys for

distancing or denying death. That is, by associating our vulnerable, biological self with more durable objects, we attempt to take the spotlight off the corruptible nature of the body. Unfortunately, the strategy backfires and the spotlight only shines ever more brightly on the frail purveyor of the illusion. The result is that we trap ourselves still further in the ego prison and, worse, in time, bequeath our material trappings to those we love most to perpetuate the folly. Sogyal Rinpoche explains this from a Buddhist perspective:

> In Tibetan ego is called *dak dzin,* which means "grasping to self." Ego is then defined as incessant movements of grasping at a delusory notion of "I" and "mine," self and other, and all the ideas, desires, and activity that will sustain that false construction. . . . The fact that we need to grasp at all . . . shows that in the depth of our being we know that the self does not inherently exist. From this secret, unnerving knowledge spring all our fundamental insecurities and fear.

Only a radical change in our outlook on life will cure these anxieties. We must start to see the world, and our relationship to it, in a very different way.

On a material level at least, physicists have been doing that for the best part of a century now. And to their surprise, they have had to come to terms with the fact that the basic physical components of nature—matter, energy, space and time—are not really what they seem to be from our blinkered human perspective. Matter is mostly empty space. Energy and matter are freely interchangeable. And space and time, which we normally think of as being distinct, are in truth inseparable aspects of a single entity, space-time. As Hermann Minkowski, one of Einstein's colleagues, wrote: "The view of space and time which I wish to lay before you has sprung from the soil of experimental physics, and therein lies its strength. It is radical. Henceforth, space by itself, and time by itself, are doomed to fade away into mere shadows, and only a kind of union of the two will preserve an independent reality."

Both the major cornerstones of contemporary physics, relativity theory and quantum mechanics, require that the three familiar dimensions of space be melded with a single dimension of time to form a four-dimensional space-time continuum. Bear in mind that this unification is not just a mathematical convenience or a piece of intellectual pie-in-the-sky. It is, our best physical theories tell us, a basic, underlying truth of the world in which we live.

From this 4-D perspective, a quite remarkable new view of reality emerges. If time is just another dimension similar to space, then the entire history of the universe from beginning to end is (and always has been) laid out along the time line. What we normally refer to as the "past" still exists, as does that part of the time line we call the "future." Our human perception of an eternal present that seems to travel along in the future direction is an illusion, fashioned by our consciousness. As the mathematician Hermann Weyl put it, "The objective world simply *is;* it does not *happen.*"

It seems that our perception of time is out of step with reality. And yet, we should not be so surprised by that. As the German philosopher Immanuel Kant first pointed out, we look out on the world with uniquely human senses and intellectual apparatus. Inevitably what we see is profoundly influenced by what we see with. And what we see with, in turn, has been conditioned and molded by biological necessity during the long course of life's evolution. We have been genetically honed over billions of years to be effective survival and reproductive systems, and part of this development has involved becoming aware of just that thin slice of reality relevant to our species' needs. In 1793 the poet William Blake wrote: "If the doors of perception were cleansed, everything would appear to man as it is, infinite." But the problem is, such all-encompassing vision would have been ruinously distracting to a slow, underpowered hominid trying to eke out a living on the dry plains of Africa. We are stuck with our particular, narrow array of sense organs and our particular subjective outlook on the world because that, as it turned out, is what served us best in the struggle to stay alive.

Among our many adaptations is this peculiar ability of our minds to perceive time as something that flows, so that we feel ourselves to be voyaging along its

course. We talk about all our experiences with reference to the present, the unique, timeless instant of
"now," and we observe things coming into being as
they enter our present awareness. But the moment of
"now" and the notion of "becoming" have no significance outside the realm of the ego-centered mind. The
French physicist Louis de Broglie, who played an important part in establishing the foundations of quantum
theory, summed up the paradox of time in this way:
"In space-time, everything which for each of us con-
stitutes the past, the present and the future is given *en
bloc* . . . Each observer, as his time passes, discovers, so
to speak, new slices of space-time which appear to him
as successive aspects of the material world, though in
reality the ensemble of events constituting space-time
exists prior to his knowledge of it."

As an analogy, imagine you are sitting in a plane that
is waiting to take off. The engines throttle up, the
plane begins to move and you see the lights by the side
of the runway flash past in sequence, just as you experience time one moment after another. After the
plane is airborne, however, you can look down and see
all the lights together—"at the same time." The impression that the lights were flowing past was an illusion created by your particular position in relation to
the thing you were observing. Oxford mathematician
Roger Penrose has written:

Consciousness is . . . the one phenomenon that
we know of according to which time needs to

134 **DAVID DARLING**

"flow" at all! The way in which time is treated in
modern physics is not essentially different from
the way in which space is treated . . . the "time"
of physical descriptions does not really "flow" at
all . . . The temporal ordering that we "appear"
to perceive is . . . something that we impose upon
our perceptions in order to make sense of
them. . . .

We have a strong sense of being a self. And we have
a powerful impression of this self moving through time.
Yet both self and time, it seems, are chimeras of the
brain. "We" are fictions trapped within a fiction of
our own making. And we, who are but make-believe
characters, wonder if there may be a storybook heaven
in which we can all live happily ever after.

We must surely try to break out of this dream—or
nightmare. If only we can pause long enough from the
daily task of building the walls of our ego-prison still
higher, we may see a better course forward. Albert
Einstein, master architect of our new 4-D vision of the
cosmos, pointed the way:

A human being is part of the whole, called by us
"Universe"; a part limited in time and space. He
experiences himself, his thoughts and feelings as
something separated from the rest—a kind of
optical delusion of his consciousness. The delusion is a prison for us, restricting us to our personal desires and to affection for a few persons
nearest to us. Our task must be to free ourselves

from this prison by widening our circle of compassion to embrace all living creatures and the whole of nature in its beauty. Nobody is able to achieve this completely but the striving for such achievement is, in itself, a part of the liberation and a foundation for inner security.

MIND OUT OF TIME

"People normally cut reality into compartments, and so are unable to see the interdependence of all phenomena. To see one in all and all in one is to break through the great barrier which narrows one's perception of reality . . ."

—*Thich Nhat Hanh, Zen master*

*I*t is no secret that human mental experience is sharply divided. There is the familiar experience of facts, objects, events, memories and self—our analytical mode—which seems to take place against a backdrop of time. And there is that other, transcendent feeling of pure awareness in which time dissolves and the perceived and the perceiver merge into an undivided whole.

In the West, we have come increasingly to revere and rely upon the rational, timebound aspects of thought. But many human groups, not so preoccupied with "progress," display a quite different outlook on life that is less materialistic, less hurried. One particular Indian culture uses the "time to boil rice" (about thirteen minutes) as its smallest unit of time measurement—it has no need of anything more precise. The natives of the Trobriand Islands, off New Guinea, and the Hopi Indians of northeast Arizona, seem not to have any linear sense of time at all. Theirs is a continuous mode of simultaneity and present-centeredness. Instead of seeing events as a causal stream arranged in order, one after the other, the Trobrianders and the Hopis tend to regard events as forming a patterned whole, with all action drawn into a single stroke. This is mirrored in the Hopi's language, in which the verbs are strangely lacking in any usual forms of tense. An event that happened a long time ago is regarded as "far away"; distances in space, in other words, are equated with distances in time.

The two different modes of human awareness—what might be called "tight-beam" and "wide-beam"—have a physiological parallel in the two different halves of the brain. Interest in the differences between the brain hemispheres was intense at the turn of the century, but then seemed to fade. It surged again strongly, however, in the 1960s and 1970s following a remarkable series of experiments by Roger Sperry and his colleagues at the California Institute of Technology.

The subjects of these experiments were people who had undergone a radical form of surgery in an effort to relieve very severe epilepsy. This procedure involved completely cutting through the corpus callosum, which is the main connecting body between the two brain hemispheres. As a cure for acute epilepsy it was a surprising success. But the patient was effectively left with two brains—and two very different brains at that.

Tests on these "split-brain" patients showed that the majority of human analytical thinking takes place in the left cerebral hemisphere. Included in this category are our advanced language skills and our ability to break the world down into separate objects and events. The left brain dominates our decisions, supplies our will and motivation and effectively makes us who we are. In contrast, the right hemisphere is an expert in spatial reasoning and seeing the world all at once, as an interconnected system. If we were to characterize society in these terms, we might say that the developed West has a mainly left-brain type of consciousness, while other, more nature-centered cultures make fuller use of right-brain modes of thought.

Individual human beings, of course, rely on both sides of their brain. Even the most committed of rationalists use their right hemisphere for controlling the left side of their body as well as for many other tasks involving memory and sensory processing. But this caveat does not take away from the fact that there is a definite functional division between the two brain halves.

In everyday situations, the left hemisphere tends to dominate. Because it has most of the key language centers, it can communicate eloquently and so serves as the brain's spokesperson. It processes things one after another, from which it follows it must be the source of our familiar notion of clock time. Most significant, it is the home of our insecure, time-harried self. The subjective experience of the left hemisphere is literally "us." It is the habitat of our ego awareness.

This brings about an intriguing, not to say potentially explosive, situation inside our head. The left side of the brain is anxious not to lose permanent control, not to relinquish the carefully nurtured feeling of self that it gives rise to. Because it also creates the illusion of linear, sequential time and can foresee its own end, it fashions myths and grasps at any evidence, however flimsy, to try to convince itself that immortality is possible. But science now speaks loudly against the survival of self after death. So the left brain finds itself in a quandary.

Meanwhile, it glances across at its shadowy, silent partner and views its unfocused workings with almost paranoid suspicion. The right side of the brain tends to be less judgmental about the stream of data it receives from the senses. It is more inclined to take the world as it comes, without breaking down or interpreting what it sees. This leads it to support states of consciousness very different from our normal, focused awareness. If the left side of the brain is a scientist and pragmatist, the right side is very much a mystic.

Because it controls language and reason, the left brain tends to assume charge most of the time. Yet despite this, it seems as if we have a powerful, innate drive to experience the radically different states of awareness involving the right side of the brain.

Young children regularly use consciousness-altering techniques on themselves and each other when they think no adults are watching. They whirl around until vertigo and collapse set in. They hyperventilate and then have another child squeeze their chest to produce unconsciousness. They choke each other around the neck to cause fainting. Such practices are found everywhere in the world and are present at such early ages—as young as two to three years old—that social conditioning cannot be a factor.

As children grow older, they learn that similar experiences can be brought about chemically, for instance by sniffing the fumes of volatile solvents found around the house. By their teenage years, large numbers of young people seek chemically induced changes of consciousness through a wide variety of illicit and medically disapproved drugs. Virtually every culture throughout history has done the same. A rare exception are the Inuit, or Eskimo, who had to wait for outsiders to bring them alcohol since they couldn't grow anything of their own.

In North America, the Athabaskan Indians of the Canadian Northwest chew birch gum to get high. According to John Bryant of the University of Alaska, this may explain the purpose of the world's oldest-known lumps of chewing gum, found in 1993 in southern Sweden. Three wads of nine-thousand-year-old chewed birch resin turned up on the floor of a hut used by hunter-gatherers on the island of Orust. Dental experts concluded that the imprints on one piece came from a fully grown person whose teeth had not yet been worn down by the stresses of Stone Age life—almost certainly a teenager. Although the gum could have been used medicinally, Bryant suspects the chewer was probably using it as the Neolithic equivalent of a joint.

The psychologist and philosopher William James was struck by the ineffable nature of a drug-induced experience. Following a session in which he breathed in a mixture of nitrous oxide (laughing gas) and ether, he wrote: "Depth beyond depth of truth seems revealed to the inhaler. The truth fades out, however, or escapes, at the moment of coming to; and if any words remain over in which it seemed to clothe itself, they prove to be the veriest nonsense."

Nevertheless, he continued, "I know of more than one person who is persuaded that in the nitrous oxide trance we have a genuine metaphysical revelation."

Dominated as it is by left-brain thinking, our society is uneasy about people going off into trances and hallucinatory intoxications. The left brain feels threatened by mystical experiences because these involve at least a temporary loss and possibly a permanent alteration of self. A person who uses drugs may "come back" changed—in effect, be a stranger to us. We fear that influence on others, especially our children. So, we have laws against possession of drugs in the first place to discourage people from getting high.

Alcohol and nicotine, of course, are the prime exceptions. We still need our legal, right-brain fix. The paradox is that, whereas we deem almost every other mind-altering substance to be morally corrupting, alcohol is so socially acceptable that we frequently toast each other's health with it, spend vast sums on its advertising and consume it copiously in public. James praised its positive effects: "Drunkenness expands, unites and says yes . . . It makes [a person] for the moment one with the truth."

More potent psychoactives, like LSD, have even been seen as doorways to a new phase of human evolution. Long before the flower children of the sixties bloomed in California, medieval peasants in Europe had felt the strange effects of "acid" from eating stale rye bread. In 1943, a Swiss chemist isolated the chemical responsible—lysergic acid—after a bout of hallucination while carrying out research on a fungus found in rye plants. Popular use of the drug soon followed. Aldous Huxley experimented with both LSD and mescaline, and in *The Doors of Perception* extolled that consciousness-expanding drugs could be used as a shortcut to mystical experience. According to Huxley, mankind was laboring under the burden of the brain—a "reducing valve" that stemmed the flow of experience. Drugs, he claimed, could relax that valve. True to his belief, Huxley took LSD on his deathbed, shortly after completing his utopian novel *Island*—the book that inspired Timothy Leary to set up his "transcendental communities."

As millions can now testify, hallucinogens undoubtedly have a major effect on our perception of the world and our self. But when does an acid trip become an altered state, and when does an altered state become a mystical experience? Drugs can have the unfortunate effect of permanently addling the brain as well as enlightening. If they have any lasting value at all, it may be in pointing the sincere seeker of truth in the right direction.

For many, that "right" direction is meditation. As one practitioner commented after taking several acid trips with the help of a doctor friend, "We mystics are used to much stronger stuff than that."

Skeptics will point to the lavish lifestyle of that most fashionable of meditation gurus, the Maharishi Mahesh Yogi. A mystic with a surprising business acumen, his slickly packaged style of transcendental meditation (TM), loosely adapted from the teachings of the ninth-century philosopher Shankara, burst on to the scene in the Sgt. Pepper era and now claims 3.5 million adherents worldwide.

To make it more appealing to Westerners, TM is dressed up as a kind of science. But the thinly veiled Hindu ceremony that precedes every initiation (to which the novice is asked to bring a piece of fruit and a flower—together with a check) reveals its true religious significance. Having offered a Vedic prayer, the TM inductor asks the subject to sit and relax with eyes closed. Then the mantra, or chant word, is given. The initiate is told that this has been carefully selected for him or her and must be kept confidential for it to remain effective. However, this is a deception. The reason for trying to keep the mantras secret is that there are only a handful of them, which anyone can find out about and thus avoid the expense of the TM sessions, most of which are padded with pseudoscientific nonsense.

The mantra having been passed on, the initiate is now told to repeat it slowly aloud. Gradually, the inductor asks for the rate of repetition to be increased and the volume decreased, until the mantra becomes literally a panting for breath. This is intentional, but few people seem to realize that they are actually being made to hyperventilate. TM initiates frequently say their first experience was the most profound, with buzzing in their ears, a great space opening up before them and a floating sensation. In fact, this is due less to any mystical influence of the mantra than it is to the physical effects of too much carbon dioxide, a known hallucinogen.

During hyperventilation—rapid, shallow breathing—the body cannot absorb as much oxygen as it needs. At the same time, the level of carbon dioxide in the blood rises. The temporal lobe of the brain is very sensitive to oxygen and carbon dioxide concentrations, and when these change, various familiar subjective effects may ensue: a feeling of peace and omnipresent love, an apparent separation of mind and body, and a vision of emptiness or a tunnel accompanied by a bright light. They are the well-known themes of the drug-induced and near-death experiences.

Hyperventilation is a common and easy way to achieve an altered conscious state. The famous Sufi dancers, or whirling dervishes, spin their way to a carbon dioxide high and a sensation of the unity of all things. As the thirteenth-century Sufi philosopher-poet Rumi wrote: "I have put duality away. I have seen that the two worlds are one. One I seek, One I know, One I see, One I call."

Young people today have made the same discovery, that by dancing to exhaustion through head-banging or rave music (often assisted by hallucinogens such as Ecstasy), consciousness is altered and the self temporarily set free. Much of music, art, dance and poetry has this as its goal, to appeal directly to the right brain and so dissolve the ego boundary created by rational thought. As Aldous Huxley remarked: "The urge to transcend self-conscious selfhood is . . . a principal appetite of the soul."

At the root of all mystical thought is the idea that self and the world as we normally see it is an illusion. We superimpose a false picture of reality due to a basic misunderstanding of the nature of things. Modern neurologists would be forced to agree. But mysticism goes further, emphasizing the importance of a state that transcends the rational, timebound mind. As the Upanishads, Hinduism's most ancient texts, say: "He [Brahman, or what we might think of as cosmic consciousness] comes to the thought of those who know him beyond thought, not those who imagine he can be attained by thought. He is unknown to the learned and known to the simple.''

The same idea of achieving enlightenment by placing one's self in a receptive, innocent state was stressed by the Russian mystic George Gurdjieff, whose quasireligious philosophy helped spawn the modern New Age culture. And, of course, Jesus too preached that ''Except ye be converted and become as little children, ye shall not enter into the kingdom of Heaven.''

The ultimate goal of mysticism is to realize the unity of self and the absolute—that ''Thou Art That,'' as the Upanishads say. Here, surely, is more than a passing resemblance to the 4-D, interconnected world model envisaged by modern science. Remarkably, through simple contemplation, mystics have reached an understanding of the deep structure of physical reality that Western science has only recently begun to appreciate.

Eastern thinking does not see time in the same way as does the Judeo-Christian tradition—as a linear progression through a world separate from God to an afterworld heaven (or hell). In the Eastern vision, time, like self, is not real. The world as we see it is not real, nor is it slowly evolving toward some state of perfection; it is perfect every moment if only we are able to realize it. Truth exists in the timeless and universal Now, the eternity of every instant—the block universe of the space-time physicist.

We have imposed a dualistic split upon reality. Only by direct insight, the mystic believes, can we see the truth that observer and observed are one. So just as scientists experiment, mystics meditate as a way of moving closer to the truth behind the world. Meditation comes in many forms, like different roads. But all lead to the same destination—enlightenment, freedom from the illusion of self, a merging with the whole.

The simplest classification divides meditation into two forms: concentrative and mindful. Concentrative methods involve focusing without stress on a particular object in view, an idea or, as in the case of TM, a mantra—a special sound, regularly repeated (usually in silence). The goal is to reach a feeling of oneness with this focus of attention and exclude all else.

In open or mindful meditation, the approach is exactly the opposite: *everything* is allowed to flow into the subject's experience but with no attempt to discriminate between thoughts, sights and sounds. The sought-for result in this case is a sense of the undifferentiated flow of existence; rather than disappearing, the world seems fresh and new, as if seen for the first time.

In both concentrative and mindful meditation, stray thoughts are not repressed or resisted but simply let go. The goal, at least in the short term, is simply to quiet the mind and stem its habit of constantly trying to rationalize what it sees. Thoughts and feelings, which might otherwise become distracting, are allowed to wash over the meditator like gentle waves and fade as naturally as they come.

In time, with increasing skill, the practitioner may notice new experiences, "higher" states of consciousness. These involve feelings of floating, great joy and an

acceptance of things as they are. The most advanced
states of all are said to coincide with a complete loss of
self-awareness and an unchallengeable sense of objec-
tivity.

Meditation, being a personal and subjective experience, is hard for scientists with their measuring instruments to penetrate. How can we know if what the
meditator says she feels is real? And, in any case, what
does "reality" mean? The whole point of meditation is
to try to break down the barrier between observer and
observed, to see things in the raw. Accordingly, it
could be argued that the mystical "all in one" experience is far more real than the mind-constructed, outwardly projected world of science. Still, it would at
least be interesting to know more about meditation
from our familiar, analytical viewpoint. And to this end
we might ask whether meditation is distinguished by its
own characteristic modes of brain activity as, for example, are sleep and normal waking thought.

In the waking brain, the frequency of electrical activity varies quite widely. But lower frequencies—less
than fourteen cycles per second—show up more when
the brain is relaxed than when it is active and alert.
One of the most distinctive patterns is the alpha
rhythm, with a frequency between eight and thirteen
cycles per second, which is normally present when a
person is resting with their eyes closed. Early research
with EEG's showed that meditators produce a lot of
alpha waves even with their eyes open.

Normally, the alpha rhythm is blocked and replaced

by higher-frequency beta waves if there is a sudden disturbance from the outside. For most people, no amount of trying to ignore, for example, a bang or a flash of light will stop the alpha waves from disappearing. But if the person is repeatedly exposed to the same stimulus, the alpha activity eventually carries on despite the disturbance. The blocking of alpha waves, in other words, seems to be a response to events that are unexpected.

By 1957, EEG's had become portable enough for two researchers, B. K. Bagehi and S. Wenger of the State University of Iowa, to haul their equipment up into the remote mountain caves of India. There they tested yogis who were highly skilled in a concentrative form of meditation.

The yogis agreed to meditate while the scientists did everything in their power to distract them. Cymbals were clashed behind the yogis' ears, lights flashed before their eyes, and their feet plunged into icy-cold water! Not only did the harassed sages remain outwardly calm but their alpha waves kept up a steady rhythm in spite of the onslaught. The results suggested they had managed almost complete sensory withdrawal.

In 1966, Akira Kasamatsu and Tomo Hirai of the University of Tokyo tested forty-eight Japanese Zen Buddhist priests and students who had been meditating for between one and twenty years. These Buddhists practiced *zazen,* a passive, mindful meditation conducted with eyes open. As they started to relax, the meditators generated rapid alpha waves. Gradually, these rose in amplitude and fell in frequency until, in some cases, they dropped to as low as six to seven cycles per second, that is, into the range known as theta waves. The most advanced meditators showed the most theta activity. Interestingly, the Zen master's classification of his students as low, medium or high skill corresponded very closely with the EEG results and not necessarily with the number of years of practice.

The researchers also tried distracting the monks by playing a repeated clicking sound every fifteen seconds. In this case, unlike the Indian yogis, the Zen Buddhists did block their alpha waves. But whereas a control group of nonmeditators quickly became dulled and habituated to the sound, eventually showing no response whatsoever to it, the meditators responded to the click just as strongly each time. Each stimulus was perceived as if it were the first.

These findings tie in remarkably well with the subjective experiences of the two forms of meditation— one excluding the sensory world, the other observing it without comment as if it were endlessly new.

More recent evidence that something unusual goes on when people meditate has come from Peter Fenwick at the Maudsley Hospital in London. In one experiment, Fenwick took electroencephalograms of half a dozen long-term Zen meditators. In each case he found that while the subjects were meditating, there was a definite increase in activity in the right hemisphere. By linking the EEG to a computer, he transformed the data for each subject into oval-shaped diagrams, one for each type of brain wave, showing where and how large was the activity. For each of the meditators, an unusually bright region showed up on the front right-hand side of the skull. "If we saw that degree of asymmetry in someone from off the street," commented one of Fenwick's team, "we'd be worried that something very abnormal was going on."

Even more dramatic results came from studying a Zen master. These showed that for tasks such as categorizing objects, for which most people use their left hemisphere, the master used his right. Furthermore, the master was astonishingly resistant to the effects of classical conditioning. "This seems to lend some support," said Fenwick, "to his claim that he lives entirely in the present, responding to everything just as it arises."

Scientists can go only so far in confirming what meditators say. They can seek out the measurable, physical correlates of the meditating state. But to progress further, they must either accept what meditators tell them or try out the experience for themselves.

There will always be a gap between what science can measure and what human beings feel. Yet everything we know about the way the two brain hemispheres work, everything psychology has taught us about the constructed nature of the world, and everything that those who have had mystical experiences tell us, point in the same direction. There is no persistent self and no true sense in which "we" exist independently at successive moments in time. Both self and "now" are fictions conjured up along the journey of human evolution—convenient fictions as far as survival goes, but with no lasting significance.

In the light of this conclusion, our long-term prospects might seem bleaker than ever. The self we so hoped might survive death is not even allowed any substance during life. There can be no hereafter for "us," both science and mysticism agree, for "we" never really existed in the first place.

And yet, even in the face of this harsh truth, not all hope is lost. There remains that one very curious, unexpected fact—in situations in which the self breaks down, *consciousness is found to expand.*

Hindus call it samadhi, Buddhists nirvana. In Buddhist teaching, self and reality are said to be like wind blowing over the surface of water. While the wind blows, the water's surface is disturbed, the "reality" it reflects continuously broken into half-truths and confusing, distorted images. But when the wind stops, the surface of the water calms and flattens, becoming a perfect mirror of the world as it is. Hence *nirvana*— "beyond wind."

In the Rinzai school of Zen, the sought-for experience is satori—a sudden, spontaneous enlightenment when self vanishes and the whole universe takes its place. Rinzai Zen uses koans to short-circuit the rational mind. Koans are terse, enigmatic texts or dialogues between master and student whose "solution" lies beyond the bounds of analytical thought. Through contemplation of a koan, the practitioner can break through the contrived nature of perceptions to the one true reality. And when this happens, consciousness *without self* begins.

The Zen masters and others who have reached this transcendent state are powerless to relate how it feels. Words and descriptions do not encompass it. As the Chinese philosopher Lao-tzu said: "He who knows does not speak; he who speaks does not know." Only by direct personal involvement can we really know what it is like to be enlightened. And most of us cannot spend the rest of our lives in meditation. We have jobs to do, children to raise, appointments to keep.

Even so, we may eventually know what it is like to lose our selves and be one with the universe. We may someday see the prison walls of our egos broken down and the blindfolds of our senses lifted. We may do this without any special effort. For the simple fact is, we shall all someday die.

THE TRUTH,
THE WHOLE TRUTH

"And see, no longer blinded by our eyes."

—*Rupert Brooke*

Most of us die only once. But the process of dying, we now realize, is complex, gradual and, in some cases, reversible. Those who have come very near to death offer us a vicarious glimpse of what to expect when our own time comes. And that glimpse is of something quite astonishing.

So much has been said and written about NDE's in the past few years that their most remarkable aspect is often overlooked. This is not the tunnel, the light or the out-of-body sensation. It is not the meeting with spirit figures or the vision of Elysian fields. All these may be peripheral details that can be explained well enough without looking beyond what happens inside the brain as the senses fail and hallucinations and memory-held images rush to take their place. No, the big surprise, the central mystery of the NDE is the reported expansion of consciousness as life shades into death.

At just the moment we would expect awareness to close down as the body's life-support systems collapse and brain function is increasingly impaired, NDEers say that they experienced startlingly heightened cognition. For them, reality seemed more real, perception more vivid than ever before. In the words of one individual who went through this extraordinary, terminal transformation: "I felt as though I was awake for the first time in my life."

Combined with this sudden growth of consciousness is a feeling of total loss of self and of timeless, all-at-onceness. Subjects struggle to capture in words what happened to them. One NDEer, speaking on Australian television, said: "I can't exactly describe it to you, but it was just all there. It was just there all at once. I mean, not one thing at one time, blinking on and off, but it was everything, everything at one time." During the same program, a scientist called John recounted: "It's as if everything was there and everybody was there; the sense was of absolute, total fulfillment. But the quite amazing thing is that I wasn't there; John vanished at that moment."

Clearly, something momentous and unforeseen is

going on in these situations. We are brought up in the West today to believe that the brain is a creator of thought, a producer—or at least an agent in the production—of consciousness. We are indoctrinated into the materialist belief that the mental world is merely a superficial, almost superfluous outgrowth of the physical. But now, in the light of NDE's, we must forcefully challenge that view. From those who have skirted death comes this extraordinary new evidence suggesting that cognition may actually broaden and become more profound at exactly the time the brain stops working. How is that possible?

An increasing number of scientists and philosophers today are trying to "explain" how consciousness comes about. Among them are influential figures such as neurologists Daniel Dennett and Gerald Edelman, philosopher John Searle, mathematician Roger Penrose and molecular biologist Francis Crick. These investigators are struggling hard to explain consciousness purely in terms of what is going on inside the brain. In their efforts they have drawn upon ideas from fields as diverse as computer science, quantum mechanics and Darwinian evolution. Penrose, for instance, believes consciousness may result from certain unusual properties of subatomic particles. Crick, of DNA fame, has argued that consciousness emerges from the binding effect of electrical oscillations in our neurons. All are ingenious theories. But in the end all fail utterly in what they set out to do—to bridge the gap between brain states and feelings. Which among these supposed explanations can say why a brain shouldn't behave exactly as it does at a physical level and yet still be entirely unconscious? Why do "we" feel like anything at all?

It is not simply that scientists have failed to explain consciousness, they have failed (in the main) to see that such an explanation is not even possible. Today's prevailing view that subjective experiences arise spontaneously when certain physical systems (such as brains and, perhaps, computers) get complicated enough is fundamentally misguided. It stems from our habit of seeing the world dualistically—as having separate subjective and objective aspects. *But in reality there is no such separation.*

Treating the universe as if it were divided does have one big advantage. It lets us isolate those parts of nature that can be explored with logic. The Renaissance scientists such as Galileo realized this more than three centuries ago. But in making the distinction, a prejudice crept in that gave priority to "primary" (i.e., objective or measurable) qualities over "secondary" (subjective or sensual) ones. From that point on, it became built into our Western outlook that the material aspects of nature were somehow more important, more basic and more "real" than feelings. From this stems today's materialist belief that the subjective side of reality *derives from* the objective. More particularly, we have come to believe that as brains evolved they gave rise, at some point, to the "secondary" quality of consciousness. It cannot be stressed hard enough that this belief is based on a misconception.

Science has its place. It has enriched human life and freed many from ill-health, pain and drudgery. It will go on to reveal more and more about the mathematical and physical relationships that exist in nature. There is no need to decry science as a pursuit. But there is a need today, as never before, to acknowledge its ultimate limitations. If science searches the universe—as it does—for certain kinds of truth, then these are inevitably the only ones it will find. Everything else will slip through the net.

Science starts from the assumption that there is a knowable logic to the universe—which there clearly is. It then strips away all aspects of the world that logic cannot tease apart, calling these subjective. There is nothing wrong with this—science couldn't progress in any other way. The mistake is to assume that this separation of objective from subjective, which *we* choose to make, reflects how things really are. It does not. And this misunderstanding is now becoming very clear as scientists go beyond their own remit and try to explain consciousness as a derivative of brain function. Their failure is no surprise.

Consciousness is not some side-effect, or epiphenomenon, of the objective world. It is an integral, irreducible part of reality. Consciousness *is* the subjective aspect of all things—the ever-present "mind" of the universe.

Mere opinion? Yes—but then so is anything we

believe in that stands above the rational world. No one can *prove* that dualism is wrong, because proof requires logic. And subjective experience, by its very nature, falls outside logic's domain. Nor is language any help in resolving this most basic of metaphysical problems. Language stems from the illusion that the world can be divided into object and subject and so is not a vehicle by which we can then show that object and subject do not really exist.

No, it cannot be proved that the dualist view of nature is wrong, any more than it can be proved it is right. But let us suspend judgment. Let us accept that it may at least be equally valid to think of the universe as being a true indivisible unity. Where does this radically reappraised view of reality lead?

If we accept that everything in the universe has a subjective aspect to it, then the brain appears in an extraordinary new light. The brain begins to look more like a regulator or an editor of consciousness—a "reducing valve," as Huxley called it. At first sight, this may seem utterly bizarre, so familiar is the idea of the brain as a maker of thought. And yet most, if not all, the major organs of the body *are* regulators. The lungs don't manufacture the air our bodies need; the stomach and intestines are not food-producers. So, if we manufacture neither the air we breathe nor the food we eat, why assume that we make, rather than regulate, what we think?

Among those who speculated along these lines is

William James. He picked up the notion from Oxford philosopher Ferdinand Schiller, who in his book *Riddles of the Sphinx* wrote:

> Matter is an admirably calculated machinery for regulating, limiting and restraining consciousness, which it encases. Matter is not that which produces consciousness, but that which limits it. It is an explanation which no evidence in favor of materialism can possibly affect. For if a man loses consciousness as soon as his brain is injured, it is clearly as good an explanation to say the injury to the brain destroyed the mechanism by which the manifestation of the consciousness was rendered possible, as to say that it destroyed the seat of consciousness.

The French philosopher Henri-Louis Bergson was also drawn to the idea that consciousness is all around us. For him, it was a force that applies intelligence to evolution. In a similar vein, controversial biologist-writer Rupert Sheldrake has argued that consciousness exists in the form of a field spread throughout space. Individual minds, he suggests, can tune in to this field and so "resonate" with one another.

Sheldrake likens the human brain to a TV set. An extraterrestrial who had never seen television before could drive itself slowly mad trying to figure out where the picture on the screen came from solely in terms of the set's hardware. We, who know how the trick is done, recognize that the TV simply picks up and selects from the complete range of broadcast signals. And we

know, too, that even if the set is turned off or destroyed, the signals carry on.

Seen as a reducing valve, the brain is a mixed blessing.
Without it, human beings would never have evolved.
The brain shields us from an awareness of every little
thing, letting through only those experiences that are
relevant to our survival. On the other hand, the brain
prevents us from being directly in touch with reality. It
is the barrier that stands between us and the limitless
potential of the universe.

The brain is the very reason we think of ourselves as
individuals. "We" are what remains after the brain has
finished sifting through and processing all of the experiences available to it—the statue left when most of
the marble block has been chipped away. The brain
is the creator of self and, therefore, of the illusion that
the universe is divided—subject from object, feeling
from fact.

It may prove humbling, but perhaps we should begin
to think of ourselves as being deprived rather than
privileged because of our exceptional power to rationalize. We may be supremely self-conscious, but for
this very reason our awareness of reality is surprisingly
limited.

As Lynn Margulis, professor of biology at the University of Massachusetts, has pointed out:

Because we are acutely conscious of the signs and
symbols of other people, we think we are conscious of everything. But we are dimly con-

scious. . . The sensory systems of all of the 30 million species with which we share this planet are all vastly greater than the few we enjoy. Microbes respond profoundly to oxygen, methane, acids, sugars, salts, lipids . . . Phototrophic and other bacteria sense infrared and ultraviolet light we can't see.

Bigger and more powerful brains may be just the thing for conjuring up complex illusions—elaborate, multicolored dreamworlds that convince the brain's owner of their authenticity. But they do precisely the opposite of making us more conscious than our fellow species. The truth is that our outsized brains serve to block and distort consciousness. All other living creatures are more conscious than us, if by this we mean that they interfere less with the totality of experience available to them. A microbe, for instance, puts up only the most rudimentary obstacles and filtering devices between itself and the outside world. This places it intimately in touch with its environment—almost one with it. Rocks, atoms, stars and such put up no resistance at all. With inanimate objects, the distinction between the individual—the self—and the unity of everything breaks down completely. So, the bewildering paradox emerges that inert matter can be considered more conscious than anything that lives, while human beings are the least conscious creatures of all!

Such a conclusion seems unreasonable. But that is only because it runs counter to the completely false picture of the world we normally uphold. *We* are the ones who invent the myth of objects and phenomena, of separation and selfhood. *None of this really exists.* Everything we experience through our rationalizing minds is an illusion. So what does it mean to say that a rock is more conscious than a person? Simply that what it is like to be a rock is the same as what it is like to be the whole universe, because outside of the human mind there is no differentiation.

We, by contrast, are extremely *self*-conscious. Our brains manufacture the most comprehensive, convincing selves in the known universe. But that necessarily implies that we are more cut off, more estranged, than the rest of nature from the underlying reality outside ourselves. Our brains, far from being prerequisites for conscious thought, reduce the ever-present torrent of total subjective experience to a carefully moderated trickle. They condense the infinite, unbroken cosmos down to a cosy, extraordinarily parochial world that seems to revolve around the individual.

Seen from a unified perspective, then, life's evolution centers very much around the evolution of self. As life-forms developed, the tendency was always to build stronger, more selective barriers between the individual and the outside world. Today, this long saga of the emergent self is retold by each of us as we develop from newborn infant to articulate child.

Margaret Donaldson, a developmental psychologist at the University of Edinburgh, sees several distinct stages or "modes" in our mind's growth. The most primitive is the point mode, occupying the first two or three months of life, when attention is taken up wholly with the here and now. Following this brief period of innocence we move farther and farther away from a state of nonjudgmental awareness. At about eight months comes the line mode, in which attention can be given to remembering selected events in the past and imagined events in the future. Our facility for labeling and for organizing our world around the illusion of passing time starts to take a firm grip on our lives. Then, at about eighteen months, comes the core construct mode—the ability to conceptualize one's self, to form general beliefs not tied to a particular perception and to build a character for ourselves. Our illusions grow, the separation of self from reality widens. Finally and gradually, we acquire the capacity to reason and to partition the world in our uniquely human way.

In retrospect, the symbolizing ego-self phase of evolution, as it has spectacularly culminated in man today, seems inevitable. How could the penetrating beam of intelligence, that survival ploy most crucial to our species, have come about without eventually leading to an extreme rationalization of the world and a firmly entrenched sense of personal observership and self-awareness?

In all this, the development of language has been central. Yet its effect has been double-edged. On the one hand, language frees our minds to conjecture and speculate—to ask endlessly, "What if?" On the other hand, it traps us, cutting us off from the true, frontierless universe, imprisoning us in a fallacious world of our own devising.

The brain builds models. Then these models are projected outward, creating the appearance of "things" and "happenings" beyond the senses. But these phenomena are *not* objectively real. We see only our own confabulations—sophisticated falsehoods that include elements of experience as fundamental as our selves, our perceptions of moving time and our anxiety at the prospect of death.

Why does nature play such games? Why have brains and nervous systems come about if they just serve to hold back consciousness and create fantasies? Surely, if the universe is, and always has been, "cosmically conscious," the last thing it needs is a range of biological filters and funnels by which to locally diminish it.

Questions framed like those above, however, imply that the universe somehow thinks and schemes about what to do next. But as far as we know, the universe just happens. Stars happen, planets happen. And on the surface of at least one planet, molecules happen to have stuck together in such a way that what we know as life eventually emerged. Competition began. Life-forms equipped in certain special ways survived, and so had the opportunity to pass on their successful genetic programs. Evolution continued. Brains developed because, as it turned out, they had survival value. But brains were not "invented" as a means of generating consciousness. They were not laid out so that "we" could better enjoy the world and savor its sensual delights. Brains improve the survival chances of the organic structures that encase them. They assist with the four essential *F*'s—fighting, fleeing, feeding and mating.

And they do this by restricting and rescripting consciousness to just that paltry form needed to maximize
our chances of staying alive.

Humans have been outstandingly successful in the
survival and adaptation stakes not because they are
highly conscious but for exactly the opposite reason.
We are conscious of virtually nothing outside the illusory world of our self-centered minds. Of all the limitless experiences on offer, of everything the universe
"knows," we are privy to just a single sliver of time
and an extraordinarily narrow range of distorted sensory impressions.

All our lives we are hobbled by the brain's short-
sighted self-centeredness. We are hoodwinked by false
imagery, obsessed with the importance of our selves at
the hub of it all. We try to accumulate and then cling
to possessions, loved ones, status, beliefs, life.
"We"—our inner feeling of self—is desperate to carry
on in its present form. And then what? We die anyway
and find, strangely enough, that at last we are truly
alive.

DEATH AND BEYOND

"And what shall we know of this life on earth after death? The dissolution of our timebound form in eternity brings no loss of meaning. Rather, does the little finger know itself a member of the hand."

—*Carl G. Jung*

*W*e stand at the threshold of a new understanding. If we can readjust to the idea that consciousness exists only *outside* the mental world of the brain, then death no longer appears as the ultimate tragedy. It may still be an important event—the most important in our life. But it is not the end of everything. It is no great loss. Death, however poignant, is simply the removal of the "reducing valve" in our head. With the brain out of the way, the barrier between ourselves and the universe disappears.

Death is the breaking of a spell, the waking from a

dream. In this alternative paradigm, consciousness is there all the time, all around us—in the trees, the earth, the sky, the emptiness of space. It is there waiting for us to rejoin it. Consciousness is like the world outside a bubble. From within the bubble all images seem broken and distorted. Only when the bubble breaks is the true appearance of things revealed. At death it is as if "we" move from one side of our senses to the other—from the highly filtered, highly processed world inside the brain to the true, unbounded universe, where subjective and objective coalesce. We step out of the dense fog of introverted human perception to the clear air of reality.

Those who have come close to death have, as it were, poked their noses into this greater world beyond human life. They have felt, briefly, incompletely, what it is like to be free of self and in contact with the absolute nature of things. No hallucination or fit of delirium could generate such an experience. Rather, it is ordinary life that, by comparison, begins to take on the air of unreality. NDEers need no convincing that there is life beyond human existence because, for a short while during *this* life, they have been part of it. They know the truth in a sense more intimate than anyone who has not yet been through the transformation—better than any materialist who insists on experimental proof or logic. We have to realize that there are some truths that transcend rationality, that lose their essence if we push too hard for explanations and discussion.

To understand our real nature and destiny we must bypass the analytical mind. Death achieves this in style by eliminating the brain altogether. But glimpses of the inner truth can come at any time if we are able to disconnect the mechanism of interpretation. Through meditation we can learn to put a temporary stop to analytical thought. This has been the approach used throughout the ages by mystics, who have strived to see through the illusion of the rational mind to the timeless ground of existence.

Mysticism is anathema to the hard-headed pragmatist. Those who practice Western religions may balk at it, equating it with all manner of pagan beliefs. But, in fact, mysticism has been the germ-seed of all religious faith, Oriental and Occidental. Christianity, Judaism and Islam all have an inner mystical core. It is simply that in the East, mystical techniques are practiced more openly and have been more systematically developed. Great bodies of knowledge, equivalent in authority to those of Western science, have grown up around traditions such as Tibetan Buddhism and Japanese Zen. Now, in the West, people are rediscovering these teachings and trying to fit them into a wider scheme that includes our own, more material views of the universe.

The single, simple aim of all mysticism is enlightenment, a state that goes entirely beyond rational thought to the bedrock of the universe. As Louis Armstrong once remarked about jazz, "Unless you know what it is, I ain't never going to be able to explain it to you." No explanation of mysticism, no exposition of its nature and goals can properly reach to its heart. Jung wrote: "The West frequently fails to fathom exactly the depths of the Oriental mind, for mysticism in its very nature defies the analysis of logic, and logic is the most characteristic feature of Western thought. The East is synthetic in its method of reasoning; it does not care so much for elaboration of particulars as for a comprehensive grasp of the whole, and this intuitively."

Through regular practice in meditation, the mystic seeks to break free of the chains that bind us to our selves, to dissolve the barrier separating the individual from the whole. This transcendent goal has been expressed again and again by great scientists, philosophers and religious leaders throughout the ages.

The thirteenth-century Christian mystic Meister Eckhart said: "The knower and the known are one. Simple people imagine that they should see God as if he stood there and they here. This is not so. God and I, we are one in knowledge."

The Chinese philosopher Sen T'sen explained: "When the Ten Thousand Things are viewed in their oneness, we return to the Origin and remain where we have always been."

And in the Mundaka Upanishad it is written: "As rivers flow into the sea and in so doing lose name and form, even so the wise man, freed from name and form, attains the Supreme being, the Self-luminous, the Infinite.''

The message is clear: if we can learn to see through the illusion of self now, in this life, then the "I" who can die no longer exists. Death is deprived of its victim, so that the basis for fear and sorrow of death is undermined. We become part of a much larger process—the totality of being—that has no start or end.

The scientist within us may rail at this and demand, "How can there be any sort of life after death? How can consciousness exist without a brain?" But we can see now that these questions stem from a failure to grasp the true nature of consciousness and the brain. Better surely to ask, "How can there be consciousness *with* a brain?"

Still, the scientist within us may be unconvinced: "Take away the eyes and ears and other senses, take away all the nervous system, including the brain—and what are you left with by which to see and understand and experience the universe? Without these instruments, where is the means by which reality can know about itself?"

But, again, by framing the question in this way, we have fallen into the trap. We find it so hard to break out of our parochial, self-centered mode of thought. It is true that we cannot experience anything without the brain, because "we" are the brain's principal product. But it is true also that, while the brain lives, we cannot properly be conscious. Consciousness begins only when the brain and the self have died.

Think about the eye—that fabulous product of natural bioengineering. It takes in light rays and focuses them, forming an image on the retina. Then, via the optic nerve, it conveys the information in this image to the brain. But the eye does not add to what is already there—it takes away. The eye interferes with the light rays that fall into it. First it bends them from their original paths, then it destroys them completely by absorbing them. So the eye does not help us to become more conscious of the universe. Rather it denies any possibility of knowing what reality is like by altering and blocking at the source everything it comes into contact with. We cannot be conscious of *anything* that enters the eye because all such aspects of the universe are irrevocably changed or terminated in the process of "seeing." By the time we think we know about the things we are seeing, they no longer exist!

The same is true of our other senses. By hearing, we destroy any sound that reaches our ears. By touching a surface we alter unknowably the state of every atom or molecule that meets our skin. And even this description fails to do justice to the depth of our misunderstanding because "light rays," "sounds," "atoms" and "molecules" are pure artifacts of the categorizing mind. We haven't the slightest idea as to the true nature of any of these things.

Once the brain goes to work, the possibilities for any significant level of consciousness are further removed. Signals related to aspects of the universe that no longer exist (because the senses have put an end to them) are filtered and processed and worked upon in all sorts of complicated ways until an internal picture emerges of what we take to be the outside world. Upon this picture is superimposed that greatest of all fabrications—our self. And so what we perceive in the end bears virtually no resemblance to the way reality is. We live in an artificial mental environment that has come about purely for the purposes of survival.

The brain is needed to produce consciousness, we assume. But the closer we look at this idea, the more fanciful it appears. Isn't "what it is to be a light ray" so much more than "what it is to be the distorted memory of certain aspects of a light ray that no longer exists"? How do we suppose our brains even begin to grasp a few distant half-truths about the universe unless they are drawing upon a far greater knowledge and experience *that already lies beyond* our senses?

We cannot help but think of reality in pieces. Elephants, electrons, planets, people—"thing-ness" abounds in human space. And language can be used in no other way than to emphasize and reassert this illusion of the divided whole, even when it is being used to discuss mysticism.

Due to our false concept of reality we believe that we who perceive the world and the objects of our perception are completely distinct and separate. Yet the underlying nature of mind is neither the inner perceiving subject nor the external perceived objects. It is not even a combination of the two, for that is just covert dualism. In the course of separating ourselves from what we perceive, we fracture the essential unity of reality and project upon it our own mentally constructed images, just as a movie is projected upon a blank screen.

We see the world as being full of relatively stable objects, such as trees and rocks and ourselves. But in fact there is no stability anywhere, not even for a microsecond. Only our minds create that illusion. There are no trees, only a tree-air-earth-sun-cosmos process that never stands still. There are no people, only a people-air-food-cosmos process that is forever breathing, digesting and growing, breaking down and healing itself. There are no objects or things at all, but just one great interconnected system that is the whole of reality. All the world is a living, dynamic movement, continuous change and impermanence its only genuine characteristics.

How ironic that the human brain, which we hold in such high esteem, should be the very reason "we" can never be conscious. What we take to be real is only a fantasy film playing inside our heads, with ourselves as the central character. For a while longer the film will run, before it ends and the hero vanishes. Inevitably this will happen, and so we look forward with dread to the moment when the brain must die.

And yet, our fear is misplaced. Death can be de-

feated. It can be overcome, here and now, if we confront what the end of human life means to each of us
personally. In stark terms, we must gaze into the face
of the corpse that exists inside us. And then we must
go beyond the mask, looking inward ever more deeply,
so that we become intimately acquainted with the impermanence of our self and the true nature of mind and
reality.

"I'm growing old. I'm falling apart. And it's very
interesting," wrote William Saroyan. All of "us"—
our constructed selves, as well as our bodies—eventually fall apart. We cannot avoid it. The only question
is whether we choose to begin that process of self-
dissolution willingly today or wait for it to happen by
default when we die. While we are alive, we have a
choice—between the death (or diminution) of self,
which implies the beginning of consciousness, or the
continuation of self, which means prolonging the
dream.

Even without any special effort on our part, moments arise when the self flickers from view. While
absorbed in a piece of music, perhaps, or performing a
compassionate act for another, we may temporarily
forget our sense of self. For a while, a different vision
appears of a wider world in which "we" are no longer
there. "We" disappear, too, or merge with a greater
whole, during the most intimate acts of communion—
with another person; with the earth, in seeing that
everything we do affects the delicate balance of Gaea;
and with the cosmos as a whole, in the deep "know-

ing'' that we are all made of cooled stardust, which itself came from the raw stuff of genesis.

Such transcendent moments, however, are soon pushed aside as the rational mind reasserts itself. Then they are forgotten. To hold on to an appreciation of what death means, we need to become acquainted more often and more profoundly with the timeless, selfless mind inside us. We need to start letting go, loosening our grip on the material side of life.

This can seem frightening. Our tendency is to resist change, to fight against impermanence and insecurity. Keeping our job, protecting our house and family, jealously guarding everything we ''own''—especially our selves—has become an obsession with us. How can we just let go, ease up and accept that change and dissolution are facts of life? Yet this is what we must do if we are to see through the illusions that surround us. Death will confront us with the one true reality in the end. But we have the opportunity to transform our vision of the world here and now.

All the world's major religions lay great emphasis on selfless acts. ''Love thy neighbor as thyself'' is as much a central theme of Western theologies as it is of Eastern. The common goal of all these great traditions is to limit selfishness and so prepare us for the ultimate dissolution of our timebound self at the point of death. It is no coincidence that behavior which people everywhere consider intrinsically good—generosity to our fellow humans, working for the benefit of others, valuing all forms of life—serves also to lessen our preoccupation with self and so encourage the realization that we are part of an undivided unity. Only when there is no self left is there no one who can die.

It may seem that our efforts to penetrate the mysteries surrounding life and death have taken us far from science and analytical thought. But that is inevitable, and we need not feel disturbed or guilty about it. Science alone cannot tell us what happens when we die because it is blind to too many fundamental aspects of reality. This is not a problem, providing that we realize that science is simply part of a much larger enterprise of truth seeking. Science's perennial weakness is to mistake the map for the territory.

Each of us has a fine line to tread if we are to avoid on the one hand becoming too enamored with reductionism and, on the other, falling into a counterculture of New Age irrationalism. No one, from pontiffs to professors, has a monopoly on the truth. In the end, we are all just travelers—not scientists or mystics or any one brand of thinker. By nature, we are scientists *and* mystics, reductionists *and* holists, left-brained *and* right-brained, mixed-up creatures trying to catch an occasional glimpse of the truth. The best we can do is to be tolerant of both sides of our nature—knowing that these reflect the twin aspects of the universe—and learn from whatever wisdom is offered.

In a wider context, there is a need for those who profess science to be open-minded enough to admit theology and mysticism as allies in their search for a more comprehensive worldview. Similarly, those who seek truth inwardly should be prepared to recognize the value of a more rigorous, scientific approach. We need a whole-brain attitude, an end to centuries-old dualistic rivalry. As Alfred North Whitehead once remarked: "A clash of doctrines is not a disaster; it is an opportunity."

THE BEGINNING

> "Lonely? Why had he thought that . . . For that was the one thing they could never be again. Only individuals can be lonely—only human beings. When the barriers were down at last, loneliness would vanish as personality faded. The countless raindrops would have merged into the ocean."
>
> —*Arthur C. Clarke,* Childhood's End

*D*eath awaits us, but no longer with the threat of extinction. Death may mean the end of body and brain and self. But, precisely because of that, it marks the beginning of our intimate reunion with nature—our return to a wider, timeless consciousness. In the light of this knowledge all fear dissolves. Since self is an illusion, its loss amounts to nothing. Only those aspects of us that are selfless—qualities we might put under the unifying heading of "love"—will endure.

Nor need we be anxious about facing death alone. Loneliness exists only while we are under the enchantment of self, while we remain caged in our skulls, cut off from other minds, solitary prisoners of our inner, private worlds. Death is to be welcomed, when in due course it draws near, for with it we shall be freed from our terrible isolation. It is the one event that draws us all together again, back into the single true mind of the universe. Death is not a failure or a finality, but a triumph and the start of an experience we can hardly begin to imagine in our present form.

As soon as death's true nature is widely recognized in our culture we shall be able to change our attitude toward the process of dying in others. As Elisabeth Kübler-Ross has written: "We shouldn't nail the dying to the threshold between two states of consciousness. We shouldn't prolong their lives with medication, injections and life-support machines. We should let them go. They're not going into nothingness. They're entering another state of being. We must let our dead go into that world."

Once the fear of death has been removed by the knowledge that consciousness continues on the other side, our whole outlook on caring for the dying will be permanently transformed. We will not wish to resort to the paraphernalia of needless and often painful life-prolongation, to commit so many people to spending their last days joined by tubes and wires to a mass of heartless technology. The dying will be allowed to slip away quietly, peacefully, joyfully. And we can wish them well on the voyage ahead, knowing that the only true part of them that has ever existed will live on, as it lives inside each of us today.

But we can go on to do more than just change our attitude toward death in others. We can, and should, begin preparations for our own death today. That does not mean rushing out to make wills, reserving burial plots or selecting our favorite funeral hymns—though in fact any of these material preparations could be used as a launchpad to thinking deeply about what our own death implies. Proper, spiritual preparation for death involves a dedicated search for the true nature of reality. And that, in turn, calls for a lifelong voyage of discovery into consciousness without self.

How to reach this self-less inner state? How to experience, as self melts away, the transcendent consciousness that belongs not to "us" or "now" but to everything throughout space and time?

All of us, at some peak moments in our lives, have reached briefly through to the infinite—running, spinning free through the wind as a child, sitting alone on a high mountain, or in a thousand other situations that simply happen. Materialism and the drudge of the workaday world can kill the memory of such experiences and make us cynical of the pure wonder of timeless, self-less feelings. Yet they are there for anyone to enjoy at any moment if we can only remember just how to let go.

Each to his or her own. There are many ways to break through the illusionary world of the rational mind. Prayer, charity, music, poetry—a million different roads.

One approach that might be mentioned, not because it is necessarily "better" than any other, but because it is so extraordinarily well mapped and detailed, is the preparatory method for death and dying prescribed by Tibetan Buddhism. *The Tibetan Book of the Dead* is, in effect, a manual that tells how we can consciously die.

That may seem like an extraordinary claim—that as a person goes through the various stages of death he can remain alert, keenly aware of what is happening to him. We might even be inclined to pour scorn on it. But considering the depth of our own ignorance about what happens as the brain dies, criticizing other world-views might be a hasty move. We have much to learn about death—and why not start with the wisdom that has been built up meticulously over many centuries by people who have devoted their lives to a deep study of the nature of mind and reality?

Every branch of learning, from physics to philately, has its own peculiar terminology. In Buddhism, life and death are considered to be changes in what is called the Clear Light. Birth is when the Clear Light peaks, death when it declines. As we go through the process of death, our minds shift from a gross to a subtle level. This is similar to falling into a deep sleep in which there is no awareness of hearing, seeing, smelling and so on. After a while in sleep the mind becomes slightly less subtle and we begin to have dreams. This activity of mind becomes grosser and grosser until we wake up and our gross sense consciousness begins to function. In the same way, the mind at death becomes increasingly subtle and all gross sensations and memories dissolve.

What happens next may seem fantastic. According to Buddhist belief, after a while in a kind of limbo state (known as the Bardo), a person's mind becomes associated with a union of cells in a mother's womb. As the fetus develops, the mind becomes increasingly gross as it associates more closely with the bodily senses. In other words, there is reincarnation.

How do we respond to that claim? With cries of "unscientific," "un-Christian," "unprovable"? Perhaps. But we have already discussed situations in which something barely distinguishable from reincarnation could conceivably come about by technical means. What would happen if, in the future, a person who was identical to you in every way were brought to life? Would that mean that you had, in some sense, been reincarnated? Alternatively, could you be reincarnated by having your memories and thought processes downloaded into a sophisticated computer?

We don't even have to resort to such far-fetched scenarios. The fact is, there would be very little difference between the *effect* of Buddhist-style reincarnation and the emergence, after your death, of someone whose inner experience of self was very similar to your own. We could even *define* your reincarnated self to be the baby born shortly after your death whose developing self-consciousness went on to most closely resemble your own. Inevitably, there would be such a person (even if we couldn't say who it was), and he would be the one human being in the world who, as it were, took over the baton from you.

Even in the Buddhist tradition, reincarnation is not seen as a direct continuation of a particular person or soul. In other words, it is not really you that comes back but a "different you." As the present Dalai Lama has explained: "The successive existences in a series of rebirths are not like the pearls in a pearl necklace, held together by a string, the "soul," which passes through all the pearls; rather they are like dice, one piled on top of the other. Each die is separate, but it supports the one above it, with which it is functionally connected. Between the dice there is no identity, but conditionality."

Stories are frequently told of people who claim to be able to remember incidents from past lives. Some of these involve children who, upon visiting certain places for the first time, recall obscure facts about the people who once lived there, which, it is said, are subsequently verified. Other evidence comes from adults who supposedly regress to earlier incarnations during deep hypnosis.

As with NDE's, it is difficult, without researching each case exhaustively and personally, to draw any firm conclusions. Similarly, there is no way of knowing if the infants who are "found" to be reincarnations of past Buddhist masters (including the Dalai Lama himself) have any real link with people who are now dead. How could we ever confirm such claims? Nor do we know if there is any mechanism by which fragments or traces of memories can be passed on from other lifetimes. These are problems—important problems— that await a more metaphysically inquisitive science.

* * *

Finally, we return to the claim that it is possible to remain aware as the body, the senses and the self dissolve during death. In Tibetan Buddhism this is said to be paramount if the dying person is to avoid another reincarnation or, at least, coming back in some undesirable and possibly nonhuman form. The process of dissolution can be practiced in everyday life, through meditation, so that the various stages of dying can be recognized and dealt with as they occur.

Remarkably, *The Tibetan Book of the Dead* is intended to be read aloud to a person for up to *seven weeks* after Western medicine would have pronounced him dead. The teachings of the book are believed to help guide the person through each step of his or her dissolution and the final transformation of his or her consciousness.

It has often been reported that the corpses of Tibetan Buddhist masters remain fresh and curiously healthy-looking for days or even weeks after breathing has stopped. The shading of life into death seems capable of being drawn out to an extraordinary degree, with the greatest exponents of the art of dying apparently able to exert incredible control over what is happening to them.

Sogyal Rinpoche recalls an astonishing incident following the apparent death of Lama Tseten, an old Buddhist teacher, in 1959. Barely had Tseten stopped breathing when Jamyang Khyentse, Sogyal Rinpoche's own spiritual master, entered the tent where Tseten lay, as if he had sensed what had happened. According to Rinpoche, Jamyang Khyentse looked into the old man's calm face and chuckled.

"La Gen [old Lama]," said Jamyang Khyentse, "don't stay in that state!"

He could see, I now understand, that Lama Tseten was doing one particular practice of meditation in which the practitioner merges the nature of his mind with the space of truth.

"You know, La Gen, when you do this practice, sometimes subtle obstacles can arise. Come on. I'll guide you."

Transfixed, I watched what happened next, and if I hadn't seen it myself I would never have believed it. *Lama Tseten came back to life.* Then my master sat by his side and took him through . . . the practice for guiding the consciousness at the moment of death.

We can make of this what we will. Whether we choose to look more deeply into what Buddhist traditions have to offer or whether we opt for a different mystical or religious or scientific path is entirely up to us. There are no best guides, no single right way—only a common goal.

In our lives we go through many rites of passage: birth, first day of school, first sexual encounter, marriage, birth of offspring, retirement, death. Each is a trial, a teetering moment of crisis, a leap from one state of being to another. But of them all, death is toweringly the most important.

With death comes a certain end to body and brain. With death, everything we took ourselves for is abruptly stripped away leaving . . . what? Nothing, except that which really mattered all along. Death rips through the membrane that separates "us" from the whole, undifferentiated universe.

The truth we must come to terms with, sooner or later, willingly or not, is that we do not survive beyond the grave. But, then, who did we think "we" were during life? We do not survive unchanged even from one moment to the next. The person who woke up this morning is not the same who is reading these words now. And, more to the point, the person you are now is no more than a crafty sleight of your survival-oriented mind.

For as long as we lay emphasis on the importance of self and seek to shore up our ego-awareness, death will continue to terrify us with its threat of dissolution. In every sense it is selfish to be afraid to die. Only by pursuing a life course that diminishes our obsession with self, with material and emotional "me-ness," can we gain the deeper insights needed to face death with equanimity. A wonderful future lies ahead of us, following the trial of death, but not as individuals. In store is nothing less than a grand reunion with reality, an expansion of consciousness that can only occasionally be glimpsed through the dim portals of our senses and brain.

Many questions remain. But this much is already clear: death is not the end or a mindless void. It is not a doorway leading to oblivion. It is a beginning. After death we shall all be together at last—except that, in another sense, "we" will be the only ones who are not there. What was us will have merged again with the unbroken ocean of consciousness. We shall have returned to the place from which we came. We shall be home again—and free.

"There is my truth; now tell me yours."

—*Friedrich Nietzsche*

Bibliography

Aries, Philippe. *Western Attitudes Toward Death: From the Middle Ages to the Present.* Baltimore: The Johns Hopkins University Press, 1974.

Barlow, Horace (ed.) et al. *Images and Understanding: Thoughts About Images, Ideas About Understanding.* Cambridge: Cambridge University Press, 1990.

Barrow, John. *Pi in the Sky: Counting, Thinking and Being.* New York: Oxford University Press, 1992.

Blackmore, Susan. "Are Out-of-Body Experiences Evidence for Survival?" *Anabiosis: the Journal of Near-Death Studies,* Dec. 1983.

Blum, Harold. *Time's Arrow and Evolution.* Princeton University Press, 1951.

Bohm, David. *Wholeness and the Implicate Order.* London: Routledge & Kegan Paul, 1980.

Bowker, John. *Licensed Insanities: Religions and Belief in God in the Contemporary World.* London: Darton, Longman and Todd, 1987.

————. *The Meanings of Death.* Cambridge: Cambridge University Press, 1991.

Brandon, Ruth. *The Spiritualists: The Passion for the Occult in the Nineteenth and Twentieth Centuries.* London: Weidenfeld, 1983.

Chomsky, Noam. *Knowledge of Language: Its Nature, Origin, and Use.* Westport, Connecticut: Greenwood Press, 1986.

Cook, Norman. *The Brain Code.* London: Methuen, 1986.

Cotterill, Rodney. *No Ghost in the Machine.* London: Heinemann, 1989.

Coveney, Peter, and Highfield, Roger. *The Arrow of Time.* New York: Fawcett-Columbine, 1990.

Crick, Francis. *The Astonishing Hypothesis: The Scientific Search for the Soul.* New York: Scribner's, 1994.

Damasio, Antonio R., and Hanna Damasio. "Brain and Language." *Scientific American,* Sep. 1992.

Darling, David. *Equations of Eternity: Speculations on Consciousness, Meaning, and the Mathematical Rules That Orchestrate the Cosmos.* New York: Hyperion, 1993.

David, A. Rosalie. *The Ancient Egyptians: Religious Beliefs and Practices.* London: Routledge & Kegan Paul, 1982.

Davies, Paul. *The Mind of God.* London: Heinemann, 1992.

Dennett, Daniel C. *Consciousness Explained.* London: Allen Lane, 1991.

d'Espagnat, Bernard. "Quantum Theory and Reality." *Scientific American,* Nov. 1979.

DeWitt, Bryce. "Quantum Mechanics and Reality." *Physics Today,* 23, p. 30, Sep. 1970.

Donaldson, Margaret. *Human Minds: An Explanation.* London: Allen Lane/Penguin, 1992.

Dunbar, Robin. "Why Gossip Is Good for You." *New Scientist,* Nov. 21, 1992.

Eccles, Sir John C. *Evolution of the Brain, Creation of the Self.* New York: Routledge, 1990.

Edelman, Gerald M. *The Remembered Present: A Biological Theory of Consciousness.* New York: Basic Books, 1990.

————. *Bright Air, Brilliant Fire.* New York: Basic Books, 1992.

Flanagan, Owen. *Consciousness Reconsidered.* Cambridge, Massachusetts: MIT Press, 1992.

Fulton, Robert (ed.). *Death and Identity.* New York: John Wiley & Sons, 1966.

Greyson, Bruce. "A Typology of Near-Death Experiences." *American Journal of Psychiatry,* 142, pp. 967–969, 1985.

Grof, Stanislav. *Beyond the Brain.* Albany, New York: State University of New York, 1985.

Harpur, Tom. *Life After Death.* Toronto: McClelland & Stewart, 1991.

Harth, Erich. *The Creative Loop: How the Brain Makes a Mind.* Reading, Massachusetts: Addison-Wesley, 1993.

Herbert, Nick. *Elemental Mind: Human Consciousness and the New Physics.* New York: Dutton, 1993.

Jaynes, Julian. *The Origin of Consciousness in the Bicameral Mind.* Boston: Houghton-Mifflin, 1976.

Johnson, Martin. "The Onset of Human Identity and Its Relationship to Legislation Concerning Research on Human Beings." *Ethical Problems in Reproductive Medicine,* 1, 1989.

Kapleau, Philip. *Wheel of Death: A Collection of Writings from Zen Buddhist and Other Sources on Dying-Death-Rebirth.* New York: Harper & Row, 1971.

Kübler-Ross, Elisabeth. *Death: the Final Stage of Growth.* Englewood Cliffs, New Jersey: Prentice-Hall, 1985.

Levy, Stephen. *Artificial Life: The Quest for a New Creation.* London: Jonathan Cape, 1992.

Luria, A. R. *The Man With a Shattered World.* New York: Basic Books, 1972.

Mermin, N. David. "Quantum Mysteries for Everyone." *Journal of Philosophy,* 78, p. 397, 1981.

Midgley, Mary. *Science As Salvation*. New York: Routledge, 1992.

Mirecea, Eliade. *Cosmos and History: The Myth of the Eternal Return*. New York: Harper & Row, 1959.

————. *A History of Religious Ideas*. University of Chicago Press, 1978.

Moody, Raymond A. Jr. *Life After Life*. Covington, Georgia: Mockingbird, 1975.

Morse, Melvin, and Perry, Paul. *Closer to the Light*. New York: Villard Books, 1990.

————. *Transformed by the Light*. New York: Villard Books, 1992.

Ornstein, Robert, and Thompson, Richard F. *The Amazing Brain*. London: Chatto & Windus: The Hogarth Press, 1985.

Penrose, Roger. *The Emperor's New Mind*. New York: Oxford University Press, 1989.

Reanney, Darryl. *The Death of Forever*. Melbourne: Longman Cheshire, 1991.

Ring, Kenneth. *Life at Death*. New York: Coward, McCann and Geohegan, 1980.

Rinpoche, Sogyal. *The Tibetan Book of Living and Dying*. Harper San Francisco, 1992.

Sabom, Michael. *Recollections of Death: A Medical Investigation*. New York: Harper & Row, 1982.

Sacks, Oliver. *The Man Who Mistook His Wife for a Hat*. New York: Summit Books, 1985.

Sagan, Carl. *Broca's Brain*. New York: Random House, 1985.

Schreiber, Flora Rheta. *Sybil*. New York: Warner, 1973.

Schrodinger, Erwin. *My View of the World*. Woodbridge, Conn.: Ox Bow Press, 1964.

————. *What is Life?* Cambridge University Press, 1967.

Searle, John R. *The Rediscovery of the Mind.* Cambridge, Massachusetts: MIT Press, 1992.

Shatz, Carla J. "The Developing Brain." *Scientific American,* Sep. 1992.

Sherman, Barrie, and Judkins, Phil. *Glimpses of Heaven, Visions of Hell: Virtual Reality and Its Implications.* London: Hodder & Stoughton, 1992.

Siegel, Ronald. "Hallucinations." *Scientific American,* Oct. 1977.

Smith, Anthony. *The Mind.* London: Hodder & Stoughton, 1984.

Stock, Gregory. *Metaman: Humans, Machines, and the Birth of a Global Super-Organism.* London: Bantam Press, 1993.

Storm, Rachel. *In Search of Heaven on Earth: The Roots of the New Age Movement.* London: Bloomsbury, 1991.

Weiskrantz, L. *Blindsight: A Case Study and Implications.* New York: Oxford University Press, 1986.

Wolpert, Lewis. *The Unnatural Nature of Science.* London: Faber and Faber, 1992.

Zaleski, Carol. *Otherworld Journeys: Accounts of Near-Death Experiences in Medieval and Modern Times.* New York: Oxford University Press, 1987.

About the Author

DAVID DARLING studied at the universities of Sheffield and Manchester and holds a Ph.D. in astronomy. After a spell as applications software manager for Cray Research in Minneapolis, he became a full-time freelance science writer in 1982. He is the author of more than thirty books for adults and children, including *Deep Time* and *Equations of Eternity*. He lives in the north of England with his wife and two teenage children.